MINDFUL LIVING

How to Take Life One Step at a Time

JASON HEMLOCK

MINDFUL LIVING:
How to Take Life One Step at a Time
by Jason Hemlock

ISBN: 979-8397201247

CONTENTS

Foreword v

Introduction ix

Chapter One: What is Mindfulness? 1

Chapter Two: Laying The Foundations for Being Mindful 6

Chapter Three: The Eight Attitudes and The Four Agreements 24

Chapter Four: Simple Ways to Weave Mindfulness into Your Day 30

Chapter Five: A Potential Mindfulness Routine 37

Chapter Six: Being Mindful with The People Around You 47

Chapter Seven: Mindful Exercises 53

Chapter Eight: Journaling Your Mindful Journey 74

Chapter Nine: Mindful Eating 84

Chapter Ten: Mindfulness Meditation 99

Chapter Eleven: Mindfulness Apps 118

Chapter Twelve: Mindfulness-Based Cognitive Therapy (MBCT) 123

Conclusion 128

Thanks For Reading 130

References 132

FOREWORD

As a way of saying thank you for reading this book, I'm offering a free meditation tracker to help you monitor your progress when you sign up for my email list. You will also receive updates and future content from me.

The meditation tracker includes a daily self-care checklist, a page on daily positive affirmations and a daily gratitude journal exercise. You can sign up by visiting bouchardpublishing.com/mindfulness

ALSO BY JASON HEMLOCK

The Power of Meditation:
Simple Practices for Mental Clarity and Relaxation

Stoicism:
How to Use Stoic Philosophy to Find Inner Peace and Happiness

Secrets of the Stoics:
How to Live an Undefeatable Life

Practicing Stoicism:
A Daily Journal with Meditation Practices, Self-Reflections and Ancient Wisdom from Marcus Aurelius

INTRODUCTION

Over the past couple of decades, mindfulness has gradually been increasing in popularity. Now it's used by Fortune 500 companies to improve productivity. Celebrities turn to it to keep their mental health balanced. While it might be easy to dismiss it as just another fad, science supports the fact that even if you're only mindful for a few moments every day, it can have a myriad of benefits, not least of which is to help you cope with the stress of modern living[1].

We will delve into these benefits in more detail later, but to just give you an idea of what you can expect when you're mindful, mindfulness has been shown to be as effective as drugs in treating depression and anxiety. In 2016, the Oxford Mindfulness Centre carried out a scientific review into mindfulness. It found that when patients used meditation and observed and analyzed their emotions, they were 23% less likely to relapse than those who didn't practice mindfulness. This was the case even when individuals had stopped taking antidepressants[2].

The beauty of mindfulness is that it's free. You can do it any time you like. You can be mindful all day or you can simply take a couple of minutes to give yourself a mindful break before getting back to work. It is a highly inclusive practice that can be tailored to your lifestyle and circumstances, bringing with it a multitude of benefits.

In this book you will get everything you need to live mindfully. We'll go through a range of techniques you can incorporate into your day. Choose the ones that work best for you and leave the rest. This is **your** practice, and you get to decide what it looks like. We will cover:

- The history of mindfulness
- How to know if mindfulness is right for you
- The benefits of mindfulness
- The many ways you can incorporate mindfulness into your life
- Apps for mindfulness
- Mindfulness-based cognitive therapy
- Mindfulness meditations
- Mindfulness exercises

As you travel down the path to mindfulness, you may well find your practices change. It might be that when you first start, you have to actively remind yourself to do a mindful activity and wonder how you'll be able to fully incorporate it into your life. Then one day, you discover that you're living mindfully without needing to actively take time out to devote to mindfulness.

Mindfulness has enriched my life in a profound way. It is difficult to put into words how much it has changed me for the better.

The best way to understand is for you to experience it for yourself.

Read on to discover how simple it can be to enjoy mindful living.

CHAPTER ONE:

WHAT IS MINDFULNESS?

At its core, mindfulness is simply the act of being fully focused on the present moment. You are only concerned about the now rather than reliving the past or stressing about the future. That's it! Nothing arcane or esoteric about it.

But while it's a very simple concept, many erroneously believe that it requires some form of Zen mastery to practice. In later chapters we'll go into a range of techniques you can use to bring mindfulness into your daily life. You'll see for yourself how anyone can be mindful, even children. In fact, children are naturally mindful, and we can learn a lot from them. Watch any small child play and you'll see that they are completely absorbed by what they're doing. They're not fretting about what's going to happen tomorrow or caught up in what happened a week ago. They only care about what's right in front of them. It's only when we grow that we cast aside this innate ability, but it never goes away.

Mindfulness involves being completely cognizant of what is going on both inside our mind and in the world around us. For most of us, this state eludes us. We are mind*less* rather than mindful. We're not allowing ourselves to be totally aware of what's happening in our environment. We react instinctively instead of choosing our thoughts and actions carefully with conscious control. Mindfulness means we tune into present events so we can actively decide on the best course of action.

Anyone can be mindful if they choose to cultivate these three core skills:

- Noticing events as they are occurring moment by moment, paying attention to both internal and external aspects.
- Identifying ingrained reactions to events. This may involve avoidance or overthinking.
- Developing an ability to respond to events and people with a compassionate mindset of active curiosity.

It doesn't matter how young or old you are. It doesn't matter what your background. Mindfulness is open to everyone.

A brief history of mindfulness

Modern mindfulness is free from any religious or spiritual connotations. It is compatible with whatever religious beliefs you may have, just as it is suitable for those who have no beliefs at all.

However, while it may not be explicitly spiritual, it is an ancient technique that has been used across cultures throughout the ages, either by itself or as part of a spiritual or religious practice. The ancient Greeks were no strangers to mindfulness either. Heraclitus said, 'The content of your character is your choice. Day by day, what you choose, what you think, and what you do is who you become.' This demonstrates how, when we are mindful, we can shape the person we are and make positive choices to build a better life.

You may associate mindfulness with Eastern religious and spiritual traditions, particularly Hinduism and Buddhism. However, mindful techniques can be found in early Judaism, Christianity, and Islam. It is just as much embedded into Western spirituality as it is Eastern. However, over the centuries, it fell out of favor in the West until its rebirth in Western culture during the 20th century, when people such as Jon Kabat-Zinn looked to Eastern teachers to learn about this forgotten art.

This means that what we now understand to be mindfulness has very strong roots in Eastern philosophy and spirituality.

Mindfulness in Hinduism and Buddhism

While Hinduism is believed to be the oldest religion in the world, its origins have been lost in the mists of time. It developed from several spiritual traditions in the region now known as India. It has no known individual founder, and we cannot precisely pinpoint when it was first practiced. In fact, it wasn't until the 1800s that different Vedic traditions were collected together to be known as 'Hinduism.'

One thing we do know is that mindfulness has been at the heart of Hinduism for as long as we can trace its history. Yoga is discussed in the *Bhagavad Gita*, while Vedic meditation is inherently mindful. We cannot separate mindfulness from Hinduism.

While Hinduism's origins may be difficult to determine, we know a lot more about the development of Buddhism. The movement was founded by Siddhartha Gautama, who became the Buddha, sometime around 400-500 BCE. Gautama is thought to have been born and raised in either India or Nepal, which makes it highly probable he would have learned about Hinduism. As a result, there is an element of overlap between Hinduism and Buddhism, although they are distinct from each other.

Buddhism outlines the path to enlightenment. Mindfulness, or Sati, is believed to be the first towards this, so mindfulness is woven into all parts of Buddhism. There is an argument to state that the West owes a debt of gratitude to Buddhism for mindfulness, as many of the early Western exponents of mindfulness studied Buddhist techniques before adjusting them to suit Western culture and mindset.

How mindfulness came to the West

Jon Kabat-Zinn is held up as being one of the main founders of mindfulness in the West. He established the Center of Mindfulness at the University of Massachusetts Medical School and the Oasis Institute for Mindfulness-Based Professional Education and Training.

Kabat-Zinn studied with various Buddhist teachers before putting together his Mindfulness-Based Stress Reduction program (MBSR). This brought together Eastern mindfulness with Western scientific research to create a practice suited to Western thinking. MBSR gave rise to Mindfulness-Based Cognitive Therapy (MBCT), which has been subsequently proven to be a successful treatment for depression[1]. Other mindfulness pioneers included Jack Kornfield, Sharon Salzberg, and Joseph Goldstein, who founded the Insight Meditation Society (IMS) together and played a major part in normalizing mindfulness as a helpful tool.

This fusion of science with Eastern philosophy was one of the reasons why mindfulness took hold in the West. Knowing that there was evidence for its effect, rather than just New Age hopefulness, made it easier for mindfulness to be taken seriously as a counter to the stress of modern living.

In the 21st century, there are numerous organizations devoted to mindfulness and its benefits. There is a plethora of resources available to anyone wishing to study this powerful practice. With countless studies having demonstrated that mindfulness enhances physical and mental health, many people who might otherwise question it are instead incorporating it into their daily lives and finding their lives are enhanced as a consequence. Clinical therapists use mindfulness to help their clients enjoy better mental wellbeing.

With mindfulness firmly in the mainstream, there is no reason not to try it for yourself to see how it can improve your life.

Summary

- Mindfulness involves being completely focused on the present moment.
- Mindfulness practices can be found in all major religions, but modern mindfulness has its roots in Hinduism and Buddhism.
- Mindfulness does not have to have any religious or spiritual associations.
- Jon Kabat-Zinn brought mindfulness to the West, fusing Eastern thinking with Western science to create his Mindfulness-Based Stress Reduction program (MBSR).
- Mindfulness is a well-researched science-based way of combating stress and improving physical and mental wellbeing.

CHAPTER TWO:

LAYING THE FOUNDATIONS FOR BEING MINDFUL

While being mindful simply means to be present in the moment, there are many different ways for you to do this. You can become a constant observer of your thoughts and gently pull them back to the now whenever you find them straying to the past or future, but this can be challenging if you're not used to such a high level of self-awareness.

Instead, you can use whatever technique appeals most to your ways of thinking and being. Many people conflate mindfulness with meditation but the two are not the same thing. While meditation is inherently mindful, you can be mindful without meditating. You could do yoga or meditation, but you can also be mindful while doing your daily chores by fully immersing yourself in the task at hand. You can be mindful by yourself or in a group. You can incorporate mindfulness into your spiritual practice, or it can be part of your mundane life.

No matter how busy or under pressure you are, there will be a mindfulness method you can weave into your routine to improve your wellbeing. When you combine our fast-paced modern lifestyle with the long-term traumatizing effect of the pandemic, we are all facing elevated levels of stress. Whether you're a full-time parent, a digital nomad, or an administrator working from home, or running a global corporation, it would appear that we're all increasingly unhappy[1].

One of the big reasons for this growth in misery is stress. Stress affects our overall health in many ways, including:

- Feeling constantly anxious or worried
- Being easily irritated
- Having a short fuse
- Being defensive and argumentative with loved ones
- Sleep issues
- Poor energy levels or waking up feeling fatigued even after a good night's sleep
- Having a mind that is always racing and incapable of taking a break
- Being highly critical of yourself and/or other people
- Finding it hard to get motivated
- Problems focusing
- Physical complaints including skin problems, headaches, or migraines
- Clenching your jaw or griding your teeth during sleep[2]

If left untreated, in the long term, stress can cause life-threatening conditions such as high blood pressure or heart disease. If you can't omit all the sources of stress (and let's be real – living *is* stressful!), then reducing its impact on your life will naturally improve your health, leading to greater happiness and quality of life.

Mindfulness is a recognized treatment for stress[3]. The great thing about it is that there is more than one way to be mindful. You can adapt it to suit you rather than having to adapt your life to fit mindfulness. When it comes to mental health, there is no one-size-fits-all. What helps me to be more mindful may not help you and vice versa. But that's why it's important to experiment with the various techniques until you find the combination that suits you best.

When mindfulness doesn't work

Most people find that mindfulness brings them nothing but positivity. When you approach it with the right attitude and know what to expect, it's a great way of supporting your wellbeing. But there are some people for whom mindfulness isn't suitable and can bring about some issues. I want to take a moment to make you aware of potential problems so you can be prepared and figure out whether mindfulness is right for you.

1. **Mindfulness can't cure everything**

   While research shows that mindfulness is beneficial for many mental health issues, it's not a panacea. For example, while mindfulness might help you develop the mental fortitude to cope with chemotherapy, it's not going to be able to remove the underlying cancer. It might give you strength to deal with difficult or emotional times, but if an abusive relationship is causing you stress, the only real solution is to leave. Giving mindfulness training to staff might help them be better employees, but it's no replacement for fair wages and conditions.

   Being mindful does not mean you should be expected to tolerate being treated badly. Sometimes the most mindful thing you can do is walk away. Mindfulness is a tool you can use to improve your quality of life, but don't let it be an excuse not to take action to make positive changes.

2. **Mindfulness isn't an excuse to be selfish**

You've probably heard the phrase 'self-care isn't selfish; it's essential.' And it's true. It's important you show yourself respect and develop high self-esteem, but this shouldn't be at the cost of those around you.

You can pay obscene amounts of money to learn mindfulness from a rich guru who only works with the wealthy, or those willing to put themselves into debt just to say they were there. You can if that's what works for you. But you don't *have* to. Mindfulness shouldn't be any more expensive than other behavioral therapies. After all, by the time you've finished reading this book, you'll have everything you need to be more mindful.

While the impact mindfulness can have on your life can be priceless, you don't have to bankrupt yourself to experience it. While that's not to say that attending a luxury mindfulness retreat can't be life changing, be sure that it's worth the price tag. It may be that money's better spent elsewhere.

3. **Mindfulness may lead to false memories**

The research on this is still in its infancy, so this may not be a major issue, but it's important you be aware of this potential side effect.

Some studies have found that people are more likely to form false memories after they've done a mindfulness meditation than those who allow their mind to wander instead[4]. It is unclear why this might be, although one theory is that it's due to mindfulness meditation engendering a judgment-free awareness and unconditional acceptance of reality. As such, it's possible this might make you more likely to accept a false memory as being true instead of questioning its validity.

4. **Mindfulness may cause us to let go of more than we want**
One reason for being more mindful is to clear the mind of negativity. One technique for achieving this involves stepping away from your thoughts and discarding those that appear to be harmful or negative. However, there is some evidence to suggest that this can also eliminate related positive thoughts. For example, one study found that when participants wrote a thought on a piece of paper and threw it away, it seemed to be removed from their mind as well, having less of an influence on future decisions. While this might seem to be a desirable thing, the study also found that any related positive thoughts were lost at the same time, so you may find that you're clearing your mind of more than you want[5].

   Clearing out negative thoughts to leave behind nothing but positive might seem appealing, but in reality, it's very difficult to do this. So be careful that while you're working on any negativity through your mindfulness practice, you're not wiping out the positive things about you as well.

5. **Mindfulness can encourage you to avoid tough choices**
As you now know, mindfulness is partly derived from Buddhism and Hinduism. As a result, it brings with it an aspect of detachment from the world around you, even while being focused on the moment. This is because mindfulness helps you to step away from obsessing over

your problems, whether these be trivial choices like what to have for lunch all the way through to major decisions, such as whether to stay with someone or leave, or whether you should change jobs.

In some people, this process of having a break means that instead of facing up to their problems and finding a solution, they actively avoid their issues. Mindfulness is not meant to support you to escape from reality. It is a tool to help you cope with your struggles, not run away from them.

6. **A small minority of practitioners have major side effects from mindfulness**

   In 2009, Kathleen Lustyk published a paper investigating potential side effects associated with mindfulness[6]. She found that for a small minority of people, mindfulness could cause problems, including:

   - Feeling detached
   - A sense of depersonalization
   - Psychosis
   - Delusions
   - Hallucinations
   - Elevated levels of anxiety
   - Loss of appetite
   - Sleep issues

I want to emphasize that these issues are very rare and it's highly unlikely you will experience them. However, it is still important to know that they're possible, especially if you're vulnerable or having mental health problems. If you are struggling, it is best to work with a qualified teacher or therapist who will know about potential side effects and make sure you don't suffer from them. Buddhist meditation aims to alter your sense of self and how you perceive the world around you. Given this, it's unsurprising that some people will develop feelings of dissociation and depression, even though this is counter to what most experience. If you find that mindfulness is making you feel worse rather than better, stop your practice and look for other ways to support your mental health. If possible, seek professional help from a qualified therapist. You can always come back to it when you're in a better mental place.

If you decide to work with a mindfulness teacher, don't be afraid to ask them about side effects. If they minimize them or discount them all together, it may be better for you to find someone who is more informed about mindfulness contraindications to ensure you have the best possible experience.

Now that you're aware of the potential pitfalls, you can approach your mindfulness practice with the right mindset and be on the alert for any issues.

The importance of regular practice

If you truly want to enjoy the full benefits of mindfulness, you'll need to practice it daily. For many busy people, the thought of 'having' to do anything every single day can feel overwhelming. You might find yourself coming up with excuses for why you can't be mindful, seeing it as yet another thing to add to an already overly full to-do list.

However, mindfulness is a relaxing, uplifting experience, which will make managing that to-do list much easier. While it might take some time to get into a routine when you first embark on your mindfulness journey, it will soon become something you naturally incorporate into your day. After all, if you look at your life, you'll find that there are plenty of routines already in place. You have your morning routine where you get up, get dressed, brush your teeth, brush your hair, have breakfast or your first cup of coffee, and go out to work. There are things you do every day almost without thinking about them and don't think about skipping them because you know they're important.

So it is with mindfulness. The studies into its benefits are generally based on someone practicing mindfulness for at least five weeks, so if you're unsure whether mindfulness will really help you, you need to commit to yourself that you're going to be mindful every day for at least 35 days.

Look at your current daily schedule. Maybe your days are rigidly timetabled. Maybe they're looser and you do different things every day. There'll still be some kind of structure in there, so take a moment to examine your daily activities and think about where you can best fit in ten minutes for your mindfulness. Maybe you'll get up ten minutes earlier. Maybe you'll do it at night right before you go to bed. Maybe you can include it in your lunch break. Whenever you decide to fit in your mindfulness, it'll be easier to establish a routine if you do it at the same time every day, so figure out a time that may work for you and have that as your mindfulness window. You can always change it later if it's not working for you.

If ten minutes seems like too much to start, then commit to only doing five minutes or even just two. Two little minutes can make a big difference. You can gradually extend the amount of time you take as you start noticing the positive impact mindfulness has. It really doesn't matter how much you do to start. You just need to start.

A word of caution. You probably have already experienced this, especially if you're the kind of person who likes to set New Year's resolutions. When you first start to establish a new habit, it's very exciting. You get excited about how you're going to be the best mindful person ever! You're going to be mindful ten times a day! You're going to be a mindful innovator!

Then something happens, and you miss a day. It wasn't your fault. You had a packed schedule, and you just couldn't take a moment out. However, having missed one day, when it's your usual time to be mindful the next day, you come up with an excuse not to do it. You're still recovering from how busy you were yesterday. You'll be mindful tomorrow.

Except tomorrow comes and you skip your mindful practice again. And again. And again. And before you know it, you've totally lost the rhythm and you decide mindfulness isn't for you. When really, it wasn't that mindfulness that was the issue. You didn't keep the promise you made to yourself when you started. That's okay. When you're aware that this is a possibility, you can put strategies in place to prevent it.

When you miss one session, it's easier to fall out of your routine. So, it's best if you can keep your daily practice going. Of course, life happens. There will be days when you can't do your mindful exercises for whatever reason (although once you've learned about all your options, you'll see that it's really easy to fit mindfulness into your day, no matter how busy you are). But set yourself up for success by asking yourself a few questions and answering them honestly.

- **Why do you want to be more mindful?** If you want to establish any new habit, whether it's mindfulness or anything else, it's important to dig deep into your motivations. When you identify your reason for wanting to do something, this can help you maintain your practice on those days when you're simply not feeling it.

  If you're not sure why you want to be more mindful (or you'd like to explore your motives in greater depth), one useful exercise is Seven Levels Deep. Sit down with a pen and paper (or your phone or computer if you'd rather type) and write at the top of the page, *Why do I want to be more mindful?* Write the first thing you think of.

Maybe it's because you want to feel less stressed. That's a great reason and something mindfulness can definitely help with but go deeper. Ask yourself, *Why do I want to be less stressed?* Maybe it's because you've noticed that you're yelling at your kids because you're taking the pressures of work home with you. So ask, *Why do I want to shout at the kids less?* Maybe it's because you remember your parents shouting at you and how it made you feel. As you keep digging into your reasons for wanting to feel less stressed, you may discover that underlying it all is a desire to be a better parent. You want to have strong bonds with your children and be the best parent you can be. You want to give your children the start in life you wish you'd had.

Now isn't that a far more powerful reason than just wanting to be less stressed?

Keep asking yourself *why* at least seven times to uncover the real reason you want to be mindful. When you're satisfied you've come up with your underlying motivation, write it on a piece of paper and put it somewhere you'll see it every day to remind yourself of your why. You might also like to set up a reminder on your phone, so your reason pops up when it's time for you to do your mindful exercise.

- **What is mindfulness to me?** Sometimes we overcomplicate or overthink things. This can then sabotage our efforts to change our habits. Thus, we can make it harder for ourselves to be mindful by telling ourselves it's harder than it really is. While it might be your goal to be totally present and focused every moment of the day, it really isn't necessary to be mindful. Trying to run before you can walk will make you stumble and fall. Likewise, mindfulness should not be conflated with being happy or thinking positive thoughts. Mindfulness isn't associated with any specific emotional state or way of thinking. In fact, mindfulness can help you cope when you're overwhelmed by emotion or struggling.

Mindfulness is nothing more than choosing to pay attention to the present moment. If your mind wanders, which is perfectly natural, all you need to do is gently pull it back to where you want to focus once you realize what's happening. If you're finding that you have to repeatedly bring your focus back to the present, this is a good thing. It doesn't mean you're a failure at mindfulness. You are consciously practicing it!

- **How can I stay curious?** Sometimes, our present reality isn't great. It can be painful, unpleasant, or even traumatic. Mindfulness is easy when you're in an idyllic location or savoring your favorite food, but our daily lives aren't always as tranquil. Your commute might bring you into contact with road ragers. You might find your colleagues annoying or hate your job. Your house might be a mess with noisy children running through it screaming their heads off. Why would you want to be mindful during these times?

  In fact, these are the very moments when you should be turning to mindfulness. Being unhappy with your work or home life involves a value judgment. Our minds are always judging what's going on around us and often find reality to be less than desirable. But when we are mindful about our observations, stop yearning for change, and instead approach our surroundings with a sense of curiosity, we have no idea what we might find that completely transforms our life. You might discover a new way of getting to work that avoids the regular traffic jams. Or you might try public transport and find out it's not only faster, but it also gives you time to read a book along the way. You might see an ad for a job you enjoy more or discover that your annoying college friend has been having problems at home, which has affected their attitude. You might start taking the children out to the park more so they can run off all that excess energy and make friends with another parent you meet there. The two of you discuss how hard parenting can be and arrange to get your partners to watch the children so you can go out for a coffee together.

When you stay curious, it's amazing the things you come up with to improve your life with very little effort.

- **How can I simplify my mindful practice?** A key mindfulness technique is meditation. However, you may find the thought of regularly meditating unappealing. Or it may be that you've tried meditation and didn't enjoy it.

  Now, you could spend money going to a spiritual retreat to learn meditation techniques, but you don't have to. Likewise, struggling with meditation doesn't mean there's anything wrong with you. It could well be that you needed to try a different technique, or you have misconceptions about what should happen during a meditation.

  You don't have to twist yourself into the lotus pose at sunrise as you chant a complicated mantra. You can foster a meditative mindset just by focusing on your breath for a few minutes. Meditation doesn't mean you should try to empty your mind. Your mind is designed to think, and stopping its natural function is challenging for anyone.

Instead, meditation involves choosing a point of focus and doing your best to maintain it – and not beating yourself up when your mind wanders.

I'll give you a range of meditation methods to experiment with later in this book, but if you decide you don't want to meditate at all, you don't have to. Mindfulness isn't about being an amazing meditator. It simply involves being observant, open-minded, curious, and compassionate. That's not so hard, is it?

- **When am I practicing mindfulness?** Are you only doing it when you're feeling emotional or overwhelmed? Most people are drawn to mindfulness because they want to make positive changes in their lives, but then think it's a tool they should only use when they're upset. While mindfulness is a helpful way of getting through darker times, it's a challenge to establish new positive habits when you only do them when you're feeling emotional.

  The more you are consciously mindful when you're in a good mood, the easier it will be to be mindful when you're not.

- **Do I need a support network?** Be kind to yourself. Learning to be mindful involves reprogramming a lifetime of thought patterns. It's only human for your mind to drift back to the past or worry about the future, forgetting that what's important is what's right in front of you.

  You might find it helpful to do a mindfulness course or join online discussion groups to talk about your experiences with other people who have been where you are on your journey. It's much easier to build new habits when you know you're not alone.

- **Will it help me to find a special place to meditate?** One thing that can help you develop a meditation routine is to delegate a specific place you're going to use for your mindfulness sessions. This should be somewhere you feel comfortable and safe. Where that will be will depend on your circumstances and preferences. It might be sitting upright in bed with pillows supporting your back. It might be sitting in your garden. You might have a favorite chair you love to curl up in. You might even have a corner somewhere in your home you can set aside for your mindfulness practice. Wherever you choose, you'll find that just going to that place will automatically help you go into the zone.

- **Is my routine realistic?** It's easier to start small and grow from there than it is to overcommit yourself and struggle to keep up with your routine. We'll go into what a mindfulness routine might look like in a later chapter, but whether you're doing a long session once a day or doing shorter exercises throughout the day, it's important to be consistent. Think about what you can realistically commit to and keep it fun! Mindfulness shouldn't be a chore. You should be looking forward to your mindfulness exercises rather than viewing them as something you've got to get over with so you can get on with more important things. If all you can commit to right now is one minute every day, that's absolutely fine. One minute is more than no minutes at all.

One little mindset hack you might find helpful is the phrase, "Can I just…?" If you're having a day when you're finding it hard to motivate yourself, ask *Can I just do one minute of mindfulness?* The chances are high you can! Then, once you've done that minute, you might find you're happy to keep going. If not, you can congratulate yourself on sticking to your promise to yourself that you're going to be more mindful.

When you start doubting whether you can do this, remember – they're just thoughts. If you find yourself thinking you can't possibly be mindful because you've got too much on your plate or your mind is awhirl, go back to the fact that these are just thoughts. You can pay them as much or as little attention as you want. You can choose to let your thoughts tell you what to do or you can use this as an opportunity to be mindful. Acknowledge those thoughts, question why you're having them to uncover the underlying cause, and then release them so you can focus on something else.

The benefits of mindfulness

Another motivation for incorporating mindfulness into your daily life is to understand just how much it's benefiting you. While it *does* make a difference – and quickly – those changes can be subtle. Sometimes it's only when you stop being mindful that you discover how great an impact it has had. Here are a few ways mindfulness can improve your life:

- **Mindfulness can help you be more compassionate.** Studies have shown that mindfulness can deactivate the Default Mode Network (DMN) in the brain. Sometimes known as the 'me' center, this is the part of the brain that generates that constant stream of consciousness that occurs when the mind is meandering from thought to thought without focus or direction. By slowing down this process with mindfulness, we can train the mind to be more aware of thoughts and feelings as they come up without conflating them with our identity. In theory, this detachment can enable us to connect more with the feelings of others, even if they are not the same as our own, and there have been experiments that would support this. For example, in one study, a group who had been practicing mindful meditation was more likely to give up their chair for someone with a broken foot than those who hadn't[7].

- **Mindfulness can be as effective as drugs in treating depression and anxiety.** A 2016 study carried out by the Oxford Mindfulness Centre delivered significant evidence that Mindfulness Based Cognitive Behavioral Therapy (MBCT) could help prevent relapses in patients suffering from long-term depression[8]. Patients were taught various meditation techniques and were encouraged to observe and analyze their emotions without letting them control their thoughts and behavior. Those who had received the therapy were 23% less likely to fall back into depression than those who hadn't, even after they stopped taking antidepressants.

- **Mindfulness can actively rewire your brain.** A 2011 study showed that mindful meditation can change the brain's chemistry. MRI scans of people who meditated for 30 minutes a day showed that they had experienced growth in the hippocampus (the part of the brain responsible for memory and learning) with less gray matter in the amygdala[9]. So, if you want to improve your brain's function, get meditating!

- **Mindfulness can help you stay healthy.** A 2009 study by Harvard Medical Researchers discovered that mindfulness could help combat disease[10]. They examined how meditation and mindfulness affect people on a genetic level, and the results were incredible. When we're stressed, our body produces hormones such as cortisol and adrenaline. When this occurs over a prolonged period, this can raise blood pressure, cause muscle tension, and weaken the immune system. Meditation, yoga, and mindfulness can counter this by inducing what's known as the relaxation effect. Over time, this turns off the genes that cause these problems and turns on the ones that fight them.
- **Mindfulness can make you less prejudiced.** In 2014, two University of Michigan students published a paper that suggested that regular mindfulness practices can help eliminate any subconscious negative associations we may have concerning race, sex, or other characteristics we may be prejudiced about[11]. Even if you are unaware of your prejudices, releasing these preconceived notions will help you be more compassionate when you deal with others.

By now, you should have a strong understanding of why you want to do this. You'll understand the obstacles that might come up to prevent you being mindful so you can be on the alert for them and deal with them before they become a problem.

It's time to get mindful!

Summary

- There are many different ways to be mindful. As such, you can choose the practices that suit your lifestyle and mindset.
- There are some negative side effects associated with mindfulness that can impact a small minority of practitioners. Having an awareness of these will help you avoid any problems.
- If you want to experience the full range of benefits, you should be mindful on a regular basis.
- Before you embark on your mindful journey, set yourself up for success by being honest with yourself and putting strategies in place to support your practice.
- Mindfulness can enrich your life in multiple ways. These can be a motivation for you to keep going on days when you don't feel inspired to be mindful.

CHAPTER THREE:

THE EIGHT ATTITUDES AND THE FOUR AGREEMENTS

Some mindful teachers like to use a framework to support you to be more mindful. There are two main methods that are used most often: the eight attitudes of mindfulness and the four agreements.

The eight attitudes of mindfulness

- **Have a questioning mind.** We've talked about being curious in your mindfulness practice. When you approach the world with a questioning attitude, you can transform the most familiar, mundane moments into something incredible. Think about what it was like when you went to a new country for the first time. Everything was alien, different, and *exciting.* If you can bring this attitude to your regular life, it will transform your experiences. Those boring chores that you put off because they're no fun can become something special. Maybe you hate cleaning because you know you're only going to have to do it all over again in a day or two. Instead of putting your focus there, think about how cool it is to uncover the clean surface beneath the dirt. Be excited about having a more organized house. Changing your mindset will change your life without having to change anything you do.

- **Be impartial.** Move away from placing value judgments on situations or people. Forget right or wrong, good or bad. Just accept things for what they are without categorizing them. When you step away from making judgments, you can appreciate that whatever is happening in the moment can change in the blink of an eye. As they say, this too shall pass.
- **Acknowledge things for what they are.** When you are able to view and accept whatever happens for what it is rather than how you want it to be, you can ground yourself in the moment and stay present.
- **Feel contentment.** Whatever your external circumstances, be comfortable in the moment. We can choose to feel inner peace and be content in the fact that change is constant. Whatever happens, it's not forever.
- **Maintain your composure.** When you are mindful, you are able to be in control of your emotions and reactions at all times. This allows you to be more compassionate and choose your words and deeds from a place of love instead of being a victim of your instincts.
- **Be accepting.** Whatever you are experiencing, accept it for what it is. Do not try to force a change or control your environment. Allow events to unfold as they will.

- **Be self-reliant.** Understand that you already have everything you need within yourself. Be brave enough to rely on yourself and your intuition to uncover the truth of what's happening instead of making assumptions.
- **Love yourself.** Give yourself the gift of pure, unconditional love and acceptance. Be happy with who you are, including your faults.

The four agreements

You can learn more about the four agreements in the best-selling book of the same name by Don Miguel Ruiz. I highly recommend it if you want to learn more about mindfulness and how you can use it to enhance your life.

Ruiz turned to the ancient Toltecs to compose the four agreements. The Toltecs were a Mesoamerican people who lived between 800 and 1000 BCE. There is evidence that they used mindfulness, which is an example of how old and universal this practice really is.

Ruiz teaches that there are four agreements you should make with yourself:

- **Be true to your word.** Everything you say should come from a place of integrity. This is easy in theory but harder in practice. For example, when you promise someone you're going to meet them at a certain time or you're going to do a particular task, you know that this promise is a type of contract. Most of the time, we'll do our very best to fulfil that promise.

  But how much do you work on keeping those promises you've made to yourself? How often have you said you're going to start exercising or go to an evening class, only to quit before you make any progress? Maybe you don't even get started in the first place.

Those promises you make to yourself are, if anything, even more important to the ones you make to other people. You matter. You are important. You deserve those things you promise yourself.

As Ruiz says, the only thing we have is our word. When we break a promise, we break trust. When you don't feel you can trust yourself, this opens the door to all that negative self-talk that drags you down.

Always think before you open your mouth. When you can choose your words with care, this can be your first step on the road to mindfulness. As you follow through on your vows, you progress further down that path. Never make a promise you can't keep or commit to something you can't follow up on – including to yourself.

- **Don't take anything personally.** When the ego's in control, it's easy to kid yourself that everything is about you. Someone shows up late for a meeting? They don't value your time. Someone pulls in front of you in traffic? They're out to get you.

  When you think the world revolves around you, you can become emotional and reactive. We snap back, escalate situations, make things worse.

  Instead, you need to put your ego in its appropriate context. Have the self-control to acknowledge how you're thinking and feeling but don't let that define your reactions. When someone upsets or annoys you, this is not a reason to take offense. It's a reflection of who they are and nothing to do with you. No matter what they say or do, it's not personal, even if it may appear that way. Remember this and it becomes easier to be more mindful.

- **Don't make assumptions.** This is something we go into frequently throughout this book and for good reason. Assumptions are one of the biggest ways you can undermine your efforts to be mindful. We spend a lot of energy every day to come up with assumptions about what other people are thinking or what their motives might be. These assumptions affect our reactions, yet they may not have any basis in reality. We could be making a situation worse simply because we assumed that something was the case. For example, you might be interested in joining a new club and haven't heard anything back about your application. You could assume that they don't want you to join and send a scathing email, telling them that you didn't want to be a member in the first place. Later you find out that they hadn't had a chance to review your application but had really wanted you to join. You've destroyed a potential opportunity by assuming the worst.

  When you free yourself from making assumptions, all the energy you were putting into them can be channeled in more productive directions. In addition, you don't have to waste time stressing over what other people think or do. It's just not important in your life.

- **Always be your best self.** Mindfulness is a practice. As such, you need to, well, practice it! Every day if you can. All day is even better. However, while this should be your ultimate goal, accept that there will be days when you aren't as mindful as you would have liked. Be kind to yourself at these times. You're human, after all, and mistakes are bound to happen.

Return to the first agreement. You have made a choice to be mindful. Honor this commitment by doing your best, whatever that might look like on any given day. Do that and everything else will work out.

Summary

- You might like to put a framework in place as a guideline for your mindfulness practice.
- There are two different ways you might like to establish this structure: the eight attitudes or the four agreements.
- The eight attitudes are: have a questioning mind; be impartial; acknowledge things for what they are; feel contentment; maintain your composure; be accepting; be self-reliant; and love yourself.
- The four agreements are: be true to your word; don't take anything personally; don't make assumptions; and always be your best self.

CHAPTER FOUR:

SIMPLE WAYS TO WEAVE MINDFULNESS INTO YOUR DAY

I will present more in-depth mindfulness exercises in later chapters, but I wanted to give you some little exercises you can use to ease yourself into being more mindful. This will show you just how simple this process can be and build your confidence as you start to incorporate the more involved practices.

The really good thing about these practices is that if you're struggling to find time to yourself because you have children or other family members who place demands on your time, you can involve them in these too. You don't even have to tell them that it's mindfulness. They'll just think of them as fun things you do together!

Say hello to the day every day

Smile as soon as you wake up. This might sound strange, but there are actually a lot of science-based reasons for smiling for no reason. When you smile, you use specific muscles in your face. This sends a signal to your brain that triggers the release of endorphins, dopamine, and serotonin, the so-called feel-good hormones, putting you in a good mood without you having to do anything. There is some evidence to suggest that smiling fools your brain into thinking you're happy. It turns out you can fake it till you make it!

Smiling also causes your brain to release neuropeptides, which are tiny proteins that reduce stress. In addition, it can lower your blood pressure. This is because when you smile and laugh, your heart rate rises. Then your muscles relax and your blood pressure and heart rate drop. This lowers your chance of developing heart disease. So, thinking about all the good you're doing to your physical and mental health simply by turning that frown upside down gives you even more reason to smile!

As you smile, allow yourself to fill with gratitude for all the good things that are going to happen and say out loud, "I'm going to have a good day." Taking this time to set a positive intention for the day will help ground and center you into the moment, as well as establishing a positive baseline for what's to come.

Take a mindful shower or bath

If a shower or bath is in your daily routine, this is a great way to start being more mindful. Given this is something you need to do anyway, it's a good opportunity to practice being more present in the moment.

As you wash yourself, take a moment to tune into each of your senses to see what's going on.

- How does the water feel against your skin? What's the temperature? How would you describe the sensation?

- What can you see? Gaze around your surroundings and see if you can spot any details you've never noticed. Look at your body as if you've never seen it before. We talk about knowing something like the back of your hand, but do you really know every inch of your hands? Examine them with the same sense of wonder a baby has when it first starts to explore its body.
- How does the water sound? Can you make it splash? If you're using a soap dispenser, what does it sound like when you pump soap into your hands? What about when you work up a lather? Does that make a noise?
- Does your soap or shampoo have a scent? Place it under your nose and inhale deeply. How would you describe the smell?

Keep your focus on the process of washing. If your mind drifts off to what you've got coming up later that day or you find yourself stressing about your problems, say thank you to your ego for telling you and let the thought go. You might like to imagine the thought being washed down the plughole so it can't bother you until you've finished. Then go back to your mindful experience with your senses.

Washing mindfully in this way gives you the same benefits as if you were sitting down to do a formal meditation. But it doesn't involve you having to change your routine or finding time in your busy schedule.

That's how easy mindfulness can be.

Have a coffee with yourself

Another way you can incorporate mindfulness into your morning routine is to be mindful with your first cup of tea or coffee for the day. Imagine you're sitting with a close friend, and use this as an opportunity to see how you're doing. How are you feeling? Are you in a good mood? Looking forward to the day? Feeling excited about all the possibilities ahead of you? Or are you feeling down? Worried about what's going to happen? Feeling stressed or pressured about your schedule? However you're feeling, just sit with it as a passive observer. Allow your experience to be *your* experience. This is how things are for you in this moment.

Now consider your physical feelings. Starting with your head, slowly scan your body from top to body. Notice if you're holding any stress or tension in any particular area. Or maybe you're feeling relaxed or upbeat. How does that feel in your body? Does any part of your body seem to be filled with emotion?

Once you have a full picture of what's occurring in your body and mind, take a moment to consciously move it in a more positive direction. This doesn't have to be a major change. If you're feeling depressed, this is not the time to put pressure on yourself to suddenly feel overjoyed. But what can you do to lift your mood a notch or two? How are you going to be kind to yourself today? What can you do to support yourself to deal with anything that may cause you stress? If your friend were to give you advice about what you should do, what would they say? Would you listen to them?

Smile more

We've already talked about the many benefits of smiling. You don't just have to confine it to first thing in the morning. You can start to consciously smile more throughout the day.

Don't wait for someone to smile at you. Smile at them first and start spreading the love. Put a smile on someone else's face by paying them a compliment. Start to consciously build connections in the world without any agenda. It doesn't matter whether it's a stranger you'll never see again or someone you see every day. Send out positive energy without expectation and start feeling how it improves your mood.

Be mindful in nature

There is a growing body of research to prove that being in nature has numerous benefits. If you spend two hours a week in nature (which can be spread out across different times), you can lower your blood pressure and levels of stress hormones. Your immune system improves. Your self-esteem goes up. Your nervous system calms. You feel less anxious. You feel less isolated. You become less aggressive. You feel calmer and happier[2].

That's a lot of positives for something as simple as talking a walk in the countryside.

But what do you do if you live in the heart of the city and don't have easy access to natural landscapes? You find the nature that's around you. Start being more observant as part of your mindfulness practice. You'll never know what signs of nature you'll notice as a result. Remember that all-important curious attitude.

If you have a couple of minutes to spare, you could go outside for some fresh air or simply look out the window. Gaze up at the sky. Watch the clouds floating by. Do any of them seem to be forming shapes or patterns? Are they static or moving? Moving slow or fast? Or are there no clouds at all? What shade of blue is the sky? This is a beautiful way of being mindful and giving yourself some time out to relax and reset.

If you're able to go out for a walk, start to notice any signs of nature. Maybe there's a dandelion growing from a crack in the pavement. Perhaps there are little patches of grass sprouting up you hadn't spotted before. You may see insects flying around. How many?

Are there any trees in your area? Is it possible for you to go and sit underneath one? If so, use this as an opportunity to tune into your body. What does the bark feel like against your back? Can you take your shoes and socks off and feel the grass beneath your feet? What's that like? Can you grab a handful of grass or dirt? How does that feel? Cycle through your senses and allow nature to soothe you.

Regularly taking time to connect with the nature everywhere will make it easier for you to keep your cool in stressful situations, even if you live miles away from the countryside.

End your day with mindfulness

Sleep is a fundamental pillar of health. The quality of your sleep impacts how you feel when you're awake, as well as supporting your bodily functions[3].

You can use mindfulness to set yourself up for a good night's sleep. Before you go to sleep, list three things you're grateful for that day. You can write these in a journal or simply say them to yourself.

They don't have to be major things. It could be something as simple as someone bringing you a cup of coffee at your desk or seeing a pretty flower while you were on your walk. It could just be that the sun was shining. You can even repeat the things you were grateful for yesterday if that's what comes to mind. The only important thing is you have three things that brightened your day in some way.

As you think of these three things, take a moment to relive the experience. If you want to give yourself an extra dose of endorphins, you can smile while you're remembering the good things about your day. Let all other thoughts go as you turn your focus to this moment. You have a warm, comfortable bed. You are safe in this moment. Let yourself be filled with gratitude as you relax into sleep.

Summary

- It is very easy to incorporate mindfulness into your day without needing to change your routine at all.
- Start the day with a smile to improve your mood and give yourself a shot of endorphins.
- Be mindful when you take a shower or bath. Cycle through your senses as you wash to be fully in the moment.
- Have a coffee date with yourself. Check in with your mind and body to see how you're feeling.
- Smile throughout the day to keep yourself feeling positive.
- Look at how you can find the nature surrounding you and actively take time out to appreciate it.
- Finish your day with mindful gratitude to help you get a better night's sleep.

CHAPTER FIVE:

A POTENTIAL MINDFULNESS ROUTINE

Now that you've seen how easy it can be to be mindful, let's take it a step further. I'm going to give you a sample mindful routine you can adapt to suit your lifestyle. This will show you that there are many ways you can be more mindful without having to make major changes that may feel overwhelming or hard to maintain.

Mindful mornings

When you begin your day with mindfulness, not only do you give yourself a positive start to the day, but you also know that you've ticked that mindfulness box. So, even if you don't do anything else for the rest of the day, you're going to start accruing the benefits.

- **Get up an hour earlier.** Many people who get up earlier find that this is a wonderful way to start. Being awake before anyone else is a very magical time. You have peace and quiet before the chaos of the day kicks in. You can use that time to meditate and exercise. You can journal. You can simply sit and enjoy your own company. This may be the only time you get to yourself all day, so savor it.

If you struggle to get up early, try setting your alarm 15 minutes earlier than normal to start and go to bed 15 minutes earlier so you get the corresponding extra sleep. Once you adjust to your new sleep/wake cycle, set the alarm another 15 minutes earlier. Keep doing this until you reach your ideal wake-up time.

- **Ease yourself into the day.** Don't force yourself to wake up too quickly. Definitely don't reach immediately for your phone and start scrolling! As you wake, your brain naturally passes through theta waves and alpha waves. These are the frequencies your brain experiences when you are deeply relaxed, such as during meditation. This phase is important for better problem solving, an enhanced memory, and learning new skills. If you immediately turn to your phone or start obsessing over your worries, you deny your brain this crucial transition time, which can negatively impact the rest of your day[1]. Use this time to smile, feel grateful, and set an intention to have a good day.

- **Get natural sunlight.** One of the advantages of getting up earlier is that you have the opportunity to get natural sunlight on your skin rather than artificial light. If you can, choose somewhere in your home facing the sunrise where you can go to enjoy this time in the morning. Meditating with the sunrise can be a profound experience. On top of that, it has various health benefits. Not only does sunlight support the body to make vitamin D, getting sunlight first thing in the morning can help you sleep better because it supports your body's circadian cycles (knowing when to go to sleep and wake up).[2]

- **Meditate.** Later in this book you'll find several meditation scripts you can use, as well as a list of some of the best paid and free mindfulness meditation apps. If you've found it hard to meditate in the past, it could well be you weren't using the right technique. Not everyone will resonate with all types of meditation. Watching the breath can be too passive for some people, while others don't enjoy mindful movement. You don't have to empty your mind of thought either – there are even meditations that involve actively observing these thoughts. You can meditate for just a few minutes or sit for an hour if that's what you prefer. There are no hard and fast rules when it comes to meditation.

  If you're new to meditation, a good thing about using an app to get you started is that it will guide you through the entire process. It's perfectly normal to find it hard to still your mind when you first try meditating and that's okay. Accept that this is your experience for the moment and simply sit with it. When you carve out a few minutes to establish a meditation practice, that alone is progress! See it as your chance to hit pause on the outside world and give yourself some precious you time as you prepare for the day ahead.

- **Make a healthy breakfast.** Many of us skip breakfast in the morning because we don't have enough time. When you're up earlier, you can give yourself a good start to the day with a nutritious breakfast. In a later chapter you'll learn all about mindful eating. Breakfast is a great opportunity to practice this.

Mindfulness during the day

It may not seem like it at first glance, but there are many opportunities for you to incorporate mindfulness into your daily routine.

- Drive mindfully. Driving can be an incredibly stressful experience. You have to contend with other drivers who can be unpredictable and aggravating. You may have other people in the car with you who distract and irritate you. You might be driving with small children who do nothing but bicker and scream for the whole ride – and there's no escaping them until you arrive at your destination.

  Mindfulness can be very helpful when you're driving. After all, as the driver, you should be aware of what's going on around you at all times so you can avoid hazards.

  You might like to ground into your body while you're driving. Notice how the steering wheel feels in your hands. Observe how your back is supported by the seat. Are you experiencing any discomfort?

  Pay attention to the world around you. How many cars can you see? What colors are they? How frequently are you checking the mirrors?

  Consider your mood. Are you happy or agitated? Calm or on edge? Remember, you can always use your breath to soothe yourself. Breathe in calm and peace. Breathe out stress and anger.

- If you're stuck in traffic during your commute, try doing a laughing meditation to while away the time. This involves fake laughing until you find yourself laughing for real. While you might feel silly when you start, it's a quick and easy way to give your mood a lift. Don't worry about what the other drivers will think about you. For all they know, you're listening to a comedy on the radio. Besides, it's not like you'll see them again.

- If you need a timeout from work or your family, try taking a 90-second break. Go somewhere you won't be interrupted for a couple of minutes. Set a timer on your phone for 90 seconds and close your eyes.

  Count to four in your mind as you inhale deeply. Put your focus fully on your breath. Notice how it feels as your draw air in through your nose and then follow it down your throat and into your lungs. Pay attention to how it affects your body and how it makes you feel.

  Hold the breath for a count of two then exhale for a count of four, letting yourself breathe away any stress or tension.

  If any thoughts creep into your mind, whether it be about the situation you've just left or anything else, acknowledge it and then breathe it away, returning to counting the breath.

  When you feel yourself relax, you can replace the count with affirmations. You might like to say, 'I am in the moment' with your inhale and 'I am focused on the present' with the exhale. Or you could use phrases to encourage the state of mind you want to have, such as 'I am happy' or 'I am calm.'

  Just 90 seconds of this will be enough to give you a mental reset before you go back to the rest of your day.

- Just as you did with your breakfast, you can be mindful as you eat your lunch. This is a good way of clearing the mind of all those thoughts that will have been buzzing around throughout the morning.

- Be mindful about how you use technology. So many of us spend our day glued to a computer screen, which can cause all sorts of physical ailments, not to mention its impact on our mental health. You probably know how this can affect your posture if you're not sitting upright, but there are lesser-known issues such as email apnea. This is when you breathe shallowly or even hold your breath while you're dealing with email or working or playing in front of a screen. It's estimated that up to 80% of people suffer with this. While it is unclear what causes this, it's possible it could be down to how we sit when we're working on our computer. We lean forward, which restricts the breath. We also tend to hold our breath if we're feeling excited, stressed, or are anticipating something happening, feelings often associated with receiving emails[3].

  Look at your workspace and make sure it's set up to be as healthy as possible. If you need to switch out your chair for one that will encourage a healthy posture, do so. Check your chair and equipment are at the right height for you so you can sit straight while working.

  You can also use technology to support your mindfulness practice. Set up reminders to stop and simply breathe or take a brief exercise break, such as a mindful walk.

- Reduce the overwhelm. When our to-do list gets too long, we can struggle to do anything because we're overwhelmed by how much there is to do. We then feel worse because we know the tasks are mounting, which puts us into a downward spiral where nothing gets down and our mood declines as a consequence.

Be more mindful with your to-do list. Take 15 minutes at the start of every day to review your list and prioritize the items in order of importance. Promise yourself you'll complete the top three tasks that day. If you know a task is too much for one day, make a commitment that you'll make significant progress towards finishing it. If you want to know you'll complete three tasks, you could break the bigger ones down into smaller steps and decide which ones you'll do that day.

Explore ways of organizing your time to support your productivity. Some people find the Pomodoro technique helps them to get more done. There are six steps to the process:

1. Choose the task you want to work on.
2. Set a timer for a relatively short amount of time (25 minutes is a good starting point).
3. Work on the task without being distracted or interrupted.
4. When the timer goes off, stop working and make a note on a piece of paper.
5. If you have fewer than four notes, take a short break of no longer than five minutes before putting your timer back on for 25 minutes and doing more work.
6. When you have four notes on your paper, you can now take a longer break of up to 30 minutes. Then reset your marks to zero and start all over again.

- Stop multi-tasking. Do you answer emails while you're on hold? Do you read or watch TV while you're eating? Do you listen to podcasts or audiobooks while you drive? Are you patting yourself on the back for how good you are at juggling all these tasks?

  We often tell ourselves that we're great at multitasking. We think we'll get more done if we cram as many tasks as possible into the same span of time. In fact, only around 2.5% of us can genuinely multitask effectively. The rest of us are kidding ourselves. Instead of multitasking, what's really going on is that our brain is constantly switching between tasks, which takes up a lot of energy. Far from making us more efficient, multitasking makes us less productive and increases the chances of errors[4].

  Imagine how much more effective you'd be if you were fully focused on a single task at a time. When you are mindful about the **one** thing that needs your attention in the moment, you can fully engage with what you're doing and give it your best effort.

- Look for ways to serve. There is evidence to show that giving is better than receiving. It makes us happier to spread the joy than to only consider our own happiness[5]. When you think about how you can support others, you'll find more meaning in the things you do for yourself. When you know that you're doing something to improve your little corner of the world, no matter how trivial, you'll feel motivated to continue to make positive changes. When you think about how you can support everyone's needs, everyone benefits – loved ones and colleagues alike, as well as you.

Mindful evenings

When you're home and winding down for the night, there are plenty of ways in which you can be mindful.

- You can have a mindful bath or shower, as described in the previous chapter.
- You can journal about your day. You'll find some prompts later in this book.
- Meditating before you go to sleep is a good way to prepare the mind for a good night's sleep. Usually, it is best to sit up when you're meditating so you don't go to sleep, but in this instance, you *want* to sleep. Make yourself comfortable before you start. There are lots of sleep meditations available online that are designed to help you drift off. You could even count sheep. Yes, that traditional suggestion can be a form of meditation. Visualize sheep jumping over a gate. Count ten sheep then go back to one and start again. Keep doing this until you fall asleep.

Summary

- There are many ways you can easily incorporate mindfulness into your day.
- Get up earlier and establish a morning routine using mindful activities.
- If you need a break during the day, try meditating. Even a 90-second break can help you regain focus.
- Instead of letting technology rule your life, look for ways you can use it to support your mindfulness practice. Make sure your workstation is set up in as healthy a way as possible

and set reminders to take breaks and do your mindfulness exercises.

- Reduce the overwhelm by changing how you do things. Do a daily to-do list and prioritize the most important three things to get done that day. If you need, break tasks down into smaller steps so you can feel like you're making progress on bigger jobs.
- Stop multitasking. Instead, do one thing at a time and be completely mindful about it. This will make you more efficient and productive, not less.
- Look for ways to serve. This will increase your happiness levels and also make those around you happier.
- Relax in the evening and get ready for a good night's sleep with more mindful activities such as journaling or meditating.

CHAPTER SIX:

BEING MINDFUL WITH THE PEOPLE AROUND YOU

Mindfulness doesn't have to be something you do by yourself, shut away from the outside world. In fact, you can bring mindfulness to your daily interactions with others. This will enhance your relationship with the people around you, whether they're loved ones or strangers. This is another example of how mindfulness can easily fit into your day without you needing to take time out or going to any extra effort. People don't even have to know you're being mindful – but they'll definitely notice the improvement in how you relate to them.

Give your full attention to others during conversations

Be honest with yourself. When you're having a conversation with someone, are you paying attention to them or are you thinking about what you want to say next? When you're in a meeting, are you listening to what's going on or have you zoned out, thinking about what you're going to do at the weekend?

Much as it's understandable to not be completely present when you're in a boring meeting, you could be missing out on important details by not being fully present. You can do this by:

- Observing non-verbal cues. Eighty percent of communication is non-verbal so when you consciously notice someone's body language, you gain a deeper understanding of what they're trying to say.
- Asking open-ended questions to encourage the other person to go into more detail.
- Paraphrasing what you were just told to show you understood what was said. This helps avoid miscommunications because if you misheard, it gives the other person to explain what they meant.
- Listening to understand what the other person is saying rather than simply waiting for it to be your turn to speak.
- Setting aside judgment and not offering advice unless asked.
- Being totally engaged in what the other person is saying.

Actively listening to what's happening around you will help you understand problems and situations in greater depth. It helps you establish trust with those around you, which encourages them to open up more, leading to better relationships. It will show others that you're interested in learning more about them and what they have to say, which will result in more positive discussions.

If you're mindful in your conversations at work, it will make you a better employee, which has the potential to bring more opportunities your way. If you're mindful in your conversations at home, it will make you a better partner or parent.

There are no downsides – only positives – to being more mindful when you're dealing with others.

Accepting the people around you for who they are

I bet there are people you know who you wish were different. You may not like how negative they are. You may wish they got to the point instead of telling you a long, tangential story every time they want to give you information. They may just have really annoying little habits that bug the heck out of you.

Whatever it is that they do that irritates you so much, it's time to let it go. You cannot change or control anyone else. The only person you can change or control is you. The sooner you can accept your reality for what it is rather than wishing it would change, the happier you'll be.

So, when someone annoys you, take a moment to check in with yourself. Notice your frustration. Observe where you feel it in your body. Acknowledge it so you can let it go. If you have a chance to go and take a few minutes to yourself, breathe it away, inhaling calm and peace and exhaling stress and tension.

If you can't leave and will need to be with that person, after you've consciously connected with your response, you can try counting your breaths in your mind. Count to ten and then go back to the start and count to ten again until you feel grounded and centered.

You will find that, as you start to manage your responses to the people around you and react in a more controlled, reasoned fashion, your interactions with them will change. Because you are not being as aggressive or emotional when you deal with them, you'll find that they will be less annoying in return.

People respond to our energies. As mindfulness supports you to shift your behaviors, you'll find that you're naturally more patient with others and it's easier to accept them for who they are, regardless of whether you like them or not.

See things from the other person's perspective

Practice being more empathetic when faced with a challenging situation. We often assume the worst of others and then tell ourselves that this assumption must be the truth instead of recognizing it's just a thought. So, for example, when someone doesn't immediately respond to a message we've sent them, we think it's because they're avoiding us, or we've done something to upset them. Most of the time, we're simply not that important. It's far more likely that the reason we haven't heard back is because they're busy with something else or they lost internet connection. Or somebody snaps at us for seemingly no reason, and we assume that they're a nasty person when, in fact, they're going through a messy divorce and didn't get much sleep the night before. That doesn't mean that they were right to treat you that way, but when you know why someone is acting the way they are, it becomes easier to have compassion for them.

Next time you find yourself making a negative assumption about someone, observe your thoughts and remind yourself that they are just thoughts. Then ask yourself, what's the best possible explanation for their behavior instead? As you start exploring alternative motives for why people do what they do, you'll find it easier to be more compassionate and understanding, which will make dealing with difficult personalities less stressful.

Take charge of your own feelings

Mindfulness does not mean that you have to beat yourself up if you have a negative thought or are having a bad day. You're still human. You can be mindful and still experience a full range of emotions, including anger, frustration, sadness, and fear. But when you are mindful, you can pause to reflect on those emotions before you react to an external stimulus, so you respond with control rather than acting out of instinct.

After all, not everyone has a high degree of self-awareness. Even if you do, it is still a journey. There's always more to discover about yourself.

So, when you're faced with something that really frustrates you, do not react immediately. Breathe deeply. Inhale through your nose and out through your mouth to calm and focus your mind. Identify how you feel and then decide if you want that feeling to dictate your words and actions.

While emotions are useful signals to tell us how we feel about something, they're not always helpful in shaping responses. You do not have to be a slave to your emotions. Just as your thoughts are simply thoughts, you can also observe your emotions and decide whether they are supporting you in the moment or not.

Be kind to others – and yourself

Have you heard the saying, *In a world when you can be anything, be kind*? It's common sense that if you are kind towards others, you're spreading a little happiness which often comes back to you. We get a warm, fuzzy feeling when we're kind to others, so we benefit by being kind as much as those on the receiving end. Kindness also helps us to keep things in perspective and engenders a sense of belonging, so we don't feel quite so isolated[1].

But while it's easy to be kind to those around you, we often forget to be kind to ourselves. If someone were to speak to us the way we often speak to ourselves, we wouldn't want to have them in our lives. We often tell ourselves we're not good enough, that we shouldn't try to pursue our dreams because we'll fail, that other people are so much more deserving than we are.

As you become more conscious of your thoughts, you can begin to change your inner dialog to a more positive one. Everyone has problems, regardless of whether you see them or not. Comparing yourself to someone else's journey is a complete waste of time.

Start being kinder to yourself. When you catch yourself saying something negative about yourself, stop. Replace that statement with a more positive affirmation, like *I am deserving,* or *I am worthy.*

We're all just doing our best to try and get through this thing called life. What you're doing is good enough, even if it may not always feel like it.

Summary

- Being mindful with those around you can enhance your relationships.
- Devote your full attention to someone during a conversation. This will make communication easier and help you have a better understanding of them.
- Accept the people around you for who they are. You cannot change others. The only person you can change is yourself. The more you work to improve yourself the more you'll discover your relationships improve as a natural consequence.
- Try to see things from other people's perspective. Begin to assume the best of them rather than the worst.
- Take charge of your own feelings. While you do not have to try to be positive and happy all the time, understanding that your emotions are just emotions will help you realize that they do not have to affect you as much as you think.
- Be kind to others and yourself.

CHAPTER SEVEN:

MINDFUL EXERCISES

Now that you've seen how simple it is to be mindful in your daily routine and with the people around you, we can dig into some specific activities you can incorporate into your new mindful way of being. These are good for those times when you feel like doing something specifically devoted to mindfulness rather than being mindful in your daily activities.

The COAL approach

This technique was first developed by Daniel Siegel in his book *The Mindful Brain*. Siegel stated that there are two ways you can deal with negative behaviors: reactive or responsive. Most of the time, we're in reactive mode. We act from a place of instinct without thinking. This can lead to negative reactions, which often escalate situations.

If you choose to be responsive, things are very different. You are able to stay calm and come up with the most positive response possible. This builds understanding and fosters greater bonds between individuals.

You can use this with your children when they're getting on your last nerve. You can use it with your partner or spouse to strengthen your connection. You can use it with colleagues for more productive working relationships. It's a straightforward process and as you get used to implementing it, you'll find that it's a simple way to resolve problems.

COAL stands for:

- **Curiosity.** When you notice someone behaving in a negative way, ask yourself why they might be doing this. Remember to assume the best of them. Think about all the possible explanations for their behavior and consider the fact that it probably has nothing to do with you at all.

- **Openness.** Do not try to force a change in the behavior. Take it for what it is and be open to it having a purpose. This is an opportunity for you to understand the other person to a greater degree.

- **Acceptance.** As you accept the behavior without trying to change it, you now have an opportunity to look for ways to handle the situation that will lead to the most productive outcome for everyone involved.

- **Love.** Allow your reaction to be shaped by kindness, compassion, and love.

You can also use the COAL approach as an intellectual exercise to become more observant of others. When you're with someone you'd like to try the COAL approach with, take a few deep breaths to center and ground yourself and then just watch them for a while. Observe their behavior without judgment. Think about how you experience them with each of your senses. What are they saying and why might they be choosing the specific words they do? Are they making any noise? What's their body language like? How are they moving? What's their facial expression? What are they focused on?

Now imagine what it would be like to be in their position. Question what might really be going on here. What might they be thinking? What are they communicating with their words and actions? Continue to observe without judgment or making any assumptions. When they directly address you, respond with that all-important attitude of kindness, compassion, and love. Then notice how that makes you feel.

Stop, Breathe, Notice, Reflect, Respond (SBNRR)

This is an alternative to the COAL approach and can be used any time you're in a difficult situation. It's a way to remember to wait and reflect before responding to what's going on around you to enable you to be aware of what you're thinking and feeling so you can formulate the most effective reaction.

As the name would suggest, there are five steps to this process:

1. **Stop.** Before you even think about doing anything, stop. This pause will prevent your emotions taking charge so you aren't controlled by your instincts and can instead be conscious and mindful in your response.

2. **Breathe.** Take a long, slow, deep breath through your nose. Hold it for a moment, then exhale slowly through your mouth. This will support you to stay calm and clear your thoughts, so your thinking isn't muddled.

3. **Notice.** Pay attention to how you're currently feeling. What emotions have arisen? Where do you feel them in your body? Is there any part of your body demanding your attention or holding onto stress, nerves, or anger? Do you feel like your emotions are overwhelming? Would it be appropriate to respond with those emotions?

4. **Reflect.** What precisely has triggered this reaction? Is this a fair or reasonable response? Do you feel like someone is deliberately targeting you? Do you feel like what's happening is a personal attack? Is that assumption reasonable? Is it definitely based in fact? Would it be possible for you to distance yourself from that opinion so you don't take what's going on personally? Remind yourself that you can't control someone else's behavior. What they are doing has absolutely no bearing on who you are as a person.

5. **Respond.** Now that you've gained a full understanding of what's going on inside you, you can explore your options in a rational manner. What are all your choices? There will be multiple ways to deal with the situation, some better than others. Which is your kindest option? You may decide to pick a different approach, but it's always a good idea to make it a habit of at least considering what would be kindest before you dismiss it. Then, once you've thought about all your possibilities, you can make an active choice about how you're going to respond. You stay in control instead of allowing the situation to control you.

This might sound like it's a long and involved process when you're caught up in a difficult situation, but in reality, it doesn't take anywhere near as much time as you think. If you can't remember all the steps, that's okay. If all you do is stop and breathe for a second or two, it will still help you be more mindful and considered in your response.

The more you use SBNRR, the faster you'll be able to process it until it becomes second nature to quickly scroll through all the possibilities before choosing what you feel is the best way forward. As with all other mindfulness practices, the more you do it, the easier it becomes.

Active listening

We've touched upon active listening earlier in this book. It's a skill that can be learned, just like any other. The more you do it, the more it becomes your default way of listening. This is a way of practicing it in a relaxed environment so you can improve your listening skills.

You'll need someone to do this with. This could be your partner, a friend, or even your children. You'll be surprised at how much you can learn from this simple exercise about the other person. As they see the impact active listening has, they may be inspired to start doing it too, which will make your communications even smoother and more effective.

The other person needs to choose a subject – any subject they like – and talk about it for three minutes without interruption. For some people, especially children, this can be difficult, so if the person speaking runs out of things to say, don't push them to say any more. Just use what they've said for the exercise.

As they talk, your job is to do nothing but listen to their words. Do not think about responding. Do not question the veracity of what they're saying. Just listen and when they're finished, repeat back as much as you can remember about what you just heard.

Doing this disrupts our usual habit about thinking about what we're going to say when someone is talking. When all you have to do is receive, you open yourself up to completely appreciate what the other person is saying. This will make you a better listener, which in turn will make you a better partner, parent, or colleague. When someone knows that you're willing to listen properly to them, it makes it more likely that they'll confide in you in the future. This will not only enhance your communication, but it will also build stronger ties between you.

Even if you only ever do this exercise with one person, you'll find that it has a knock-on effect elsewhere in your life. If you're a good listener to your spouse, you'll be a better communicator in the workplace. When you have to make a phone call to solve a problem, you'll be able to get the situation dealt with more efficiently because you'll pay attention to what the other person is telling you they can do.

If you want to take this exercise to a deeper level, you can consider what the other person is communicating to you beyond their words. What emotions do they seem to be feeling in the moment? Sadness? Happiness? Excitement? Worry? Curiosity? Anger?

When they've finished talking and it's time for you to sum up what you heard, you can also tell them the emotions you observed. There are times when we dismiss what someone else is feeling, even if we don't mean to. We might tell them they've got nothing to be upset about or that they shouldn't get angry with you. This may well be true, but that doesn't change how someone else is feeling and it isn't your job to try and control their emotions.

Another way of practicing active listening is to team up with someone you trust and can be honest with. Each of you should come up with one thing that's worrying you and one thing that makes you happy or excited. Once you've decided on what you want to talk about, take turns to go into detail about the subjects you've chosen.

When the other person is speaking, pay close attention to how they're communicating, both verbally and non-verbally. Pay just as much attention to their body language as you do their words. Does it support what they're saying or is it suggesting there's something else going on?

Be mindful of your own thoughts and feelings. Are you giving all your focus to what they're saying or are you really thinking about what you want to tell them when it's your turn?

Give them as long as they need to talk about their topics and when they're finished, repeat back to them what you heard to confirm you were listening properly. Then ask them how there were feeling when they were talking about something stressful and how it was different from when they were telling you something positive.

Now switch places. You get to talk about your two subjects and have your partner listen to you. They should also tell you what they heard and ask you how you were feeling during the process.

When you've finished, set aside some time to debrief. Talk about how you were feeling when you were listening and compare it to what it was like when you were talking. Did you feel any different? Was it easy to concentrate on what you were doing, or did you find your mind wandering? What kind of thoughts were you having, if so? What helped you to come back to the present moment? Did any unexpected emotions come up for you? Did you feel anything in your body while you or they were talking? How were you feeling before you told the other person your story? Was there a shift in your emotions after you'd finished? How are you both feeling now?

When you acknowledge how someone is feeling and you show that you understand it (even if you don't agree), it helps them feel validated. When you combine that with having properly listened to the words they've used, it offers them the rare gift of being fully heard. You can then choose whether you want to do something to meet their needs instead of simply dismissing them out of hand.

How powerful is that?

Tune in to your five senses

This is a good exercise to do sporadically throughout the day to track how you're feeling at any given moment. You might like to set a reminder on your phone so you do this regularly, or you might simply do it when the mood takes you. It involves cycling through your senses and accepting what they're feeling without judgment.

1. **List five things you can see.** Gaze about and randomly pick five things you can see. With each item, look at it with fresh eyes, as if you've never seen it before. Pay attention to its color and shape. Can you tell what the texture might be just by looking at it? How does the light fall upon it? Where are the shadows on the object? Examine it in minute detail as if you were going to be tested on it later.

2. **List four things you can hear.** There are sounds going on around us all the time, but we tune most of them out so we don't become overwhelmed. This is a chance to listen deeper, to hear those sounds that are usually filtered out, like the ticking of a clock, the sound of traffic outside, even the sound of your breath. Try to observe these quieter noises rather than the obvious louder ones like people talking or the television or radio.

3. **List three things you can feel.** What is your body in contact with? What do you have against your skin? You could do this

exercise while you're working, so you might feel the computer keyboard beneath your fingertips. Maybe you notice the sensation of the air brushing against your skin. Perhaps there's a gentle breeze you hadn't noticed. What are you wearing? How do your clothes feel on your body? Are you wearing shoes? Socks? Going barefoot? You could consider how the chair is supporting you and where your body is in contact with it, or tune into the soles of your feet to think about how they feel against the ground. Can you tell which parts of your feet are touching the ground and which are slightly raised?

4. **List two things you can smell.** We often ignore our sense of smell unless there's a particularly strong scent in the room. Even then, we can tune it out after a while, so it no longer bothers us. Close your eyes and inhale deeply. What two odors can you pick out? Are they nice or nasty? Are there people around you? What do they smell like? Is there food in the room you can smell? Do you have a drink like tea or coffee? Does that give off an aroma? Are there flowers nearby that are changing the smells in the room?

5. **List one thing you can taste.** If you haven't recently eaten or drunk anything, you may think there's no taste in your mouth, but even when your mouth's empty, you will still be able to taste *something,* even if it's the absence of taste. What's that like? Is there a lingering residue from something you consumed earlier? What does your mouth feel like right now? Is it dry or is there an abundance of saliva?

Once you've finished running through your senses, get back to your day.

Give yourself some love

You should make time every day to treat yourself to some loving kindness. You'll find a script for a loving kindness meditation later in this book, but if you don't have enough time to do the full meditation, this is a beautiful way of showing yourself love. It's a particularly good exercise to do if you've caught yourself being judgmental of yourself or thinking negative thoughts about yourself. As you become more mindful of your thoughts, you'll start to notice when you could be more loving towards yourself.

Make yourself comfortable, preferably somewhere you won't be disturbed for a few minutes. Inhale deeply, hold the breath for a moment, and then slowly exhale. As you breathe out, imagine you're ridding your body and mind of any tension or negativity.

Name whatever emotions you're feeling in the moment. Flag any thoughts you may be having. Acknowledge these thoughts and feelings and thank them for bringing these ideas to your attention.

Slowly scan your body from the top of your head down to your feet and become aware of any parts where you may be holding tension or feeling discomfort. Send breath down to that area and breathe it away until you feel calm and relaxed all over.

Close your eyes (if you haven't already) and place your hands on your heart. Inhale deeply again, imagining your body is filling with loving kindness.

If you're not used to being kind to yourself, this might be a difficult exercise for you. You may find it helpful to pretend that you are sending this support to a friend who just happens to live in your body as you become more comfortable with accepting love.

Take as long as you need to inhale loving kindness while you breathe away anything that's bothering you. When you're ready, open your eyes and go about the rest of your day.

The 4-5-6 exercise

If you find the previous exercise difficult, this is another way you can show yourself a little kindness when you need to lift your mood.

Choose an affirmation that represents how you want to feel or supports you emotionally. You can use the same one every time you do this exercise, or you can change it according to how you feel. Affirmations are first-person positive statements phrased in the present tense. So, you might choose to say to yourself, "I am loved," "I am safe," "I am supported," or "Everything is working out for my greatest good."

Put your hands on your heart and inhale for a count of four. As you do, say your affirmation in your mind.

Hold your breath as you count to five.

Count to six as you exhale, saying to yourself, "I love, honor, and accept myself just as I am."

Repeat this 4-5-6 count two or three times (or as many times as you feel you need to shift your mood), then open your eyes.

Go for a walk

While sitting still and concentrating on a point of focus like your breath or a mantra is a great way to meditate, not everyone connects with this technique. Even if you do, there may be times when your mind is running a million miles a minute and you simply can't get into the zone. If this is the case, you might find that mindful movement will help you enjoy the benefits of meditation.

The good thing about walking is that you can do it wherever you are. If you're at work, you could do a mindful walk from your office to the printer. If you're at home, you could walk from one end of the house to the other. You could walk around your garden. You could take a trip to a local park or beauty spot. Being out in nature will give you all the extra benefits associated with a calming environment, but don't worry if that's not accessible to you in the moment. The focus here is on the meditative aspect of moving rather than your location.

As you walk, allow yourself to fully ground and connect with your body. You may find yourself naturally walking more slowly, but if not, that's okay. Let your experience be your experience and let your body move how it wants to.

Observe your current emotional and mental state without judgment. Simply take a baseline of how you feel right now. Then turn your attention to your hearing and let that be your guide. Try to pick out those sounds you would normally overlook. Maybe it's the sound of the leaves rustling in the breeze. Perhaps there's a bird singing you hadn't noticed. Maybe there's a plane flying overhead, and you can hear the sound of the engine in the distance. Your feet might make a noise as you're walking. What's that like? Are there dry leaves crunching beneath your feet? Is there a squelching when you walk through mud? If you're on carpet, is there a gentle sound that's barely noticeable until you try to hear it?

Completely immerse yourself in the moment as you walk for as long as you want. Then, when you're done, think again about your emotional and mental state. Has it changed at all? How?

Mindful movement

Dancing is another form of mindfulness. When we dance for the sheer joy of moving our bodies, we're completely lost in the moment. We don't worry about whether people are watching us or what they think. We let go and our body expresses our mood.

If you're not used to dancing, this is a very easy way of letting yourself get connected to your body without worrying about how coordinated you are. Put on some music you love and let your hands tell the story of the music. Imagine someone was watching and couldn't hear the tune. Let your hands express the music so that that person would be able to know what it sounded like just by watching you.

As you let your hands move however they will, watch them as if you'd never seen them before. Think about a baby looking at its hand and feet. They're an endless source of entertainment because they're new and exciting! Bring that same sense of wonder to your sight as you watch your hands dance and let yourself be entranced by the miracle of movement.

Be quiet

You'll need the support of any people around you to do this one. If you have young children, you might like to involve them by turning this into a game of who can be quiet the longest. Turn off screens and television. People talking in movies count as chatter! If this really isn't possible, get up earlier to have your moments of silence, or wait until everyone has gone to bed so you don't have to engage with them.

Set a timer for five minutes and have everyone go about their usual business without speaking. Keep your thoughts to yourself and experience what it's like to do your regular activities without talking about them.

Initially, you might find it surprising to notice just how loud your thoughts can be when you're in a quiet environment. Don't try to silence or censor your thoughts. Let them rise and fall without judgment. As you adjust to being in silence, that inner distraction will also diminish. When you remove extraneous noise from your environment, you'll be able to connect with your other senses more so you can be more mindful about what's really going on around you.

As you get used to practicing this exercise, gradually build the amount of time you spend in silence until you can have a full hour of total quiet.

Be curious with new food

You might like to journal each stage of this exercise. If you have someone you can do this exercise with, even better. Choose a food that has strange or interesting features, like chewy chocolate chip cookies, crunchy celery, smelly cheese, or exotic lychees. Share it with your partner and instruct them to pretend they've never tried it before. (If you've chosen an unusual food, they may not have!)

Both of you should examine what the food looks like, gazing at it from all angles. Touch it with your fingertips and roll it between your fingers to explore the texture. Bring it up to your nose and inhale the scent. Does your body respond to it? In what way? Finally, put it in your mouth and chew slowly and mindfully, noticing the taste and texture and how they change while you eat.

As you explore the food with each of your senses, talk about what it's like with your partner or write your experiences in your journal. While you're paying close attention to the food, you may find that your mind sometimes drifts off to think about other things. If so, gently pull your focus back to the food, perhaps by using a different sense to examine it.

Use your eyes

Guided visualizations are a common form of meditation, and they can be highly effective. However, not everyone can see things in their mind's eye. If you are one of those people, know that there's nothing wrong with you. It's just the way your brain is wired, and you think in different ways. You might find this exercise a good alternative.

All you need is access to a view. It doesn't have to be in the countryside. It doesn't even have to be an attractive view. You just need to be able to look out across a landscape of some kind. You could do this exercise looking out of a window if you're not out and about somewhere interesting.

Make yourself comfortable and set a timer for five minutes. Now simply look around at everything you can see. Try not to name the items you spot. Instead of thinking to yourself, *there's a cloud, there's a building,* or *there's a person,* consider the colors, shapes, light, and shadow you can see. Observe what's static and what's moving. Are the clouds drifting across the sky? Is there a car moving across your vision? Are there trees moving in the breeze?

Even if this is a view you've seen countless times before, try to look at it as if you're seeing it for the first time. After all, it will never look exactly the same. Things are always changing. What's different this time? Can you see anything you haven't noticed before? Keep your gaze passive and leave judgment behind. Look at everything before you and avoid fixating on anything specific. Allow your focus to slowly drift around you so you can fully observe your surroundings.

If you find your mind wandering, acknowledge the thought, let it go. Look for something particularly interesting to draw you back to the task at hand. Observe your surroundings until the timer goes off.

If you don't enjoy looking at views, or you find it difficult to find a fresh perspective, an alternative is for you to find a natural item, like a leaf, flower, or pebble. Hold it in your hand and really look at it for five minutes. Bring it close to your eyes. Hold it at arm's length. Observe it from all angles and see how the colors change depending on how the light hits it. Consider the shape. Is it even or does it have irregularities? What can you tell about the texture from the way it looks?

See how you're doing

This is a quick exercise you can use whenever you need to bring your awareness to the present moment.

- Start by making yourself comfortable. Let your mind wander to wherever it wants to go. Let whatever thoughts and feelings come into your mind flow through, but don't start obsessing on any specific thought or emotion. Just let them come and go. Recognize that this is your current state of being and it can change at any time.

- When you feel you've got a strong sense of where your mind is, turn your attention to your breath. Inhale and exhale ten times. You can breathe deeply or observe your breathing in its current, natural state. Follow every part of the process. Notice how your body moves with the breath. Are your shoulders moving? Your chest? Your ribs? Your belly? Can you be aware of your lungs expanding and contracting? Just watch the breath and allow it to bring you to the present.

- Once you've counted ten breaths, focus on your entire body. Be aware of how you're feeling without judgment. Where are you holding any stress? Where is your body relaxed? As you connect with how your body's doing, you can expand your awareness to the space around you. Gaze around as if seeing it for the first time.

Take as long as you need to be present in your surroundings before you go back to your day. Remember you can do this at any time when you need to be more mindful.

Light a candle

If you have an open fire, you can use it for this exercise; otherwise, light a candle and use the flame to help you relax. Make yourself comfortable in front of the flame. Allow your eyes to defocus as you look at the flame. Choose a fixed point of focus – the wick if you're using a candle or a specific log or coal if you're in front of a fire. Then let your thoughts drift as they will. Don't try to follow any of them. Just let them come and go as they will as you stay present with the flame.

Give yourself a timeout

We put children in timeout when they're overwhelmed or need to think about what's going on as they calm down. However, have you ever considered that you could benefit from a timeout instead? If you find yourself getting frustrated or you're struggling to deal with your environment, remove yourself from the situation to reset yourself.

Go somewhere quiet and set a timer for a minute. While it's running, sit with yourself and ask, *How am I feeling right now?* Let whatever comes up in response flow through your mind without judgment or question. Immerse yourself in a stream of consciousness detailing your current state.

When the timer goes off, reset it for another minute and in this second minute, let those thoughts dissipate as you focus on your breath. Don't try to change or control it. Just take this minute to observe its flow. If any thoughts linger or come up, use the breath to send them away. You might like to imagine the thought turning into a feather and you can gently blow it out of your mind. This is an opportunity to let your mind calm down.

When the timer goes off, set it for one final minute. This time, do a body scan from your head to toes. Is there any part of you that's holding tension? Can you feel a particular emotion anywhere in your body? Is your gut tight with stress? Is your jaw clenched with anger? Wherever you notice any tension, send breath to that part of the body to calm and soothe it.

When the timer goes off for the last time, thank yourself for this timeout and then go back to your day.

Simply breathe

How many times have you been told to breathe when you're upset or agitated? Maybe you found it annoying to be told to focus on your breath. After all, breathing is something we do automatically. It's essential for life. But when we make our breathing slower and deeper, we nourish our body and spirit, relieving stress and anxiety.

Tune into your breath at various times throughout the day. This doesn't have to take any real time or effort at all. It can be as easy as paying attention to your breath as you slowly inhale and exhale three times. As you do, observe the flow of energy as the air moves in and out of your body. When you slow your breathing down, you release those natural calming hormones that help us stay grounded and centered so you can go about your business with a more relaxed approach.

When you get the opportunity, do a more involved breathing exercise. Go somewhere quiet without interruption and make yourself comfortable. If you can, sit with your back supported and your spine straight. While you might want to lie down, when you deeply relax, you may find yourself falling asleep, which is not what you want when you're meditating.

Let your body relax. If you find this difficult, you could start by tensing then releasing the muscles in your feet. Move up to your calves then your thighs and continue to move up all the way to your head. You can then tense all the muscles in your body and release them, which will make you feel much more relaxed.

Once your body is loose and calm, put your focus on your breath. Don't try to change or control it in any way. Simply watch how the air flows in and out. Is this easy for you or do you have to work to get the breath to move naturally? Watch your natural way of breathing without judgment.

Breathe through your nose as you connect with each inhalation and exhalation. Keep the body relaxed as you focus on the flow of air. With each inhale, feel your lungs filling completely. Allow your belly to expand to draw in even more air. When you have taken in as much air as possible, exhale in a controlled fashion, releasing the air as slowly as possible. Notice how your breathing slows without your even trying as you start controlling the inhale and exhale.

When you find your mind start to wander, simply pull your focus back to your breath. It doesn't matter what the thought is. It's not important right now. We are being in the moment and, in this moment, the only thing that counts is your breath. Watch how your body changes with each inhale and exhale. Know that you can control this process, holding the breath whenever you choose, slowing down the inhale or speeding up the exhale at will.

When you're ready, stop watching your breath and allow it to return to its natural cycle. Open your eyes and return to your day.

You can do this breathing exercise any time you like, but when you first start, you might find it helpful to do it at the same time every day as part of your regular routine. You could do it first thing in the morning to put you in a good mood for the day. You could do it during your lunch break to restore your focus. You could do it last thing at night to unwind before you go to sleep.

When you first start, you might only do a few minutes as you get used to breathwork. As you become more comfortable with the technique, you can increase the amount of time you spend mindfully breathing. There is no specific amount of time you need to devote to this powerful practice, but I'd recommend you try to do it for at least five minutes every day. You will find that if you do, it will help you be more mindful the rest of the time, even when you're not consciously trying. The more you do it, the easier it will be for you to drop into this meditative way of being so you can use it when you're feeling stressed or under pressure to return to the present moment and be more mindful.

Summary

- There are many exercises you can do to deepen your mindfulness practice.
- The COAL approach is a good way of staying calm when in a difficult situation.
- Stop, Breathe, Notice, Reflect, Respond (SBNRR) is an alternative to the COAL approach. It gives you a strategy you can use to be mindful about your reactions to others.
- Practice your active listening skills with a willing partner so it becomes your default mode of communication.
- Tune into your senses to be mindful in the moment.
- When you catch yourself being negative or critical of yourself, take a few moments to send yourself some love. You can sit with yourself for a few moments and imagine your body is

filling with loving kindness or you can use the 4-5-6 method to work with your breath and give yourself some love.

- Go for a mindful walk as a form of mindful movement.
- Dancing is another type of mindful movement. Try letting your hands tell the story of a piece of music and watch them move as if you've never seen them before.
- Actively set aside time for silence every day.
- Be curious with food, using all your senses to experience it.
- Find an interesting view and look at it without judgment, simply observing everything you can see. Alternatively, get a flower, stone, or leaf, and visually examine it from all angles.
- Check in with yourself by watching your thoughts, then your breath, then your body, then your surroundings.
- Light a candle and let the flame keep you focused as you allow your thoughts to come and go as they will.
- When things are getting a bit much, give yourself a time out to notice how you're feeling in the moment then use your breath to release stress and tension.
- Just breathe. This will calm and relax you in a matter of moments.

CHAPTER EIGHT:

JOURNALING YOUR MINDFUL JOURNEY

When we decide to try a new way of doing things or we want to develop a new habit, it's easy at first. We're all excited about the changes we're going to make and can't wait to experience our new, improved life. But that initial enthusiasm can soon fade away when we don't see an immediate, dramatic impact.

Mindfulness has a subtle effect. While it's possible you might experience some major breakthroughs as you become more mindful, for most people the changes are gradual, and it can take a few weeks to notice its effect.

This is where journaling can be useful.

Journaling does not have to be onerous. You don't have to sit down for hours every night and write a detailed transcript of what happened that day. It can be as quick as jotting down a few sentences at the end of the day about how you feel. You might note any specific mindful activities you did and how they changed your reactions to a situation. You could just rate your mood on a scale of 1-10.

Documenting your experiences will allow you to build up a record of your progress so that when you're feeling like it's not making any difference, you can review your journal and see that you are making progress.

Mindful journals give you an opportunity to reflect on your current thinking and pinpoint any emotional triggers you may have that mindfulness can help with. When you use journaling to explore the day's challenges and what you did in response, you can identify the approaches that work for you and the ones you need to let go. Journaling is also another opportunity to exercise self-love. Writing without agenda, censorship, or criticism supports you to accept yourself for who you are as you work on becoming the best version of yourself you can be.

Journaling has been scientifically proven to have many benefits[1]. It is used by many coaches, counselors, and therapists to support individuals with their mental health. There are two forms in particularly that are commonly used:

- **Expressive writing.** This is where you let your thoughts and feelings flow onto the page with a focus on your emotions rather than specific events on individuals. So, you could use this to explore how a mindful approach changed your response to a situation compared to what you would have done in the past.

- **Gratitude journaling.** This involves making note of all the things you are grateful for. These can be major events like a promotion or pay raise, the birth of a child, or the start of a new relationship, but they can also include the smaller things in life like a sunny day, a good conversation, or a comfortable bed. However, you should be aware that for some people, gratitude journaling every day can lose its effect because it can be difficult to maintain a sense of positive gratitude and start to feel like a chore, undermining its effect. If you find that this is true for you, you might like to have a day or two a week as your specific gratitude journaling days and use a different form of journaling the rest of the time.

Whatever type of journaling you choose, there is evidence to suggest that a regular journaling practice will help your mental health. It can:

- Lower anxiety
- Break the pattern of overthinking and obsessing over events in your life
- Regulate your emotions
- Increase self-awareness
- Improve your physical health
- Help you understand your personal needs and wants
- Reduce your blood pressure
- Enhance liver and lung function
- Cut down on the amount of time spent in hospital
- Lift your mood
- Allow you to spot when negative self-talk occurs and change that inner monolog
- Identify your triggers
- Increase your creativity
- Combat the symptoms of depression
- Lower stress
- Improve cognitive function
- Work on your communication skills
- Support you to process difficult situations
- Increase your job satisfaction

- Enable you to work through your thoughts and emotions without recrimination or judgment
- Allow you to process negative emotions in a controlled way
- Increase your grades[2]

The great thing about journaling is that you don't have to do it every day to enjoy these benefits. This means that if you skip a day, there's no need to beat yourself up about it. Just be aware that if you allow that one day to turn into two, or three, or four, it's going to be harder to get back into the habit. That's okay too. Start again – there's always another chance to develop good habits.

Mindful journaling

If you want to develop a journaling practice, you'll find it helpful to weave it into your routine at the same time every day. Journaling in the evening gives you an opportunity to look back over your day while it's still fresh in your mind. Journaling first thing in the morning allows you to set an intention for the day ahead. You could even journal twice a day or journal throughout the day when you have a free moment. If you get a bus or train to work, you could use the commute as an opportunity to journal.

Whatever time you choose, make sure you have enough time to journal without interruptions. If you're living with other people, make sure they know you need half an hour to process your day. Again, if this is hard, you might find that getting up early is the best solution.

Before you put pen to paper, take a minute to ground and center yourself. Close your eyes and take a few deep breaths. If you like, you could do a short meditation before you start writing. Establishing a journaling routine will make it something to look forward to and help you get the most out of each session.

It's a good idea to get a notebook or journal specifically for your mindfulness practice. Treat this book as something sacred and special – because it is! If you prefer, you can use your computer or phone to write out your thoughts. You could even dictate them if you like. However, there's something very profound about writing by hand, so if this is at all an option for you, I'd advise you take this approach. You may well find you enjoy it more than you expect.

Start each day's entry on a new page or document. Let the words flow and don't read what you've written until you've finished journaling. You may prefer not to read them at all. You might feel like you just need to get the ideas out and once they're on paper, you don't need to think about them again.

This is **your** journal, so the only rules are the ones you set for yourself. Have fun with it. Explore various formats to see what works for you. Here's some suggestions to get you started:

- Choose a situation that stands out to you. Write out what happened and how you responded to it. Did you use a mindfulness practice to help you cope or did you react instinctively? Remember – there's no judgment here. Simply record what happened so you can be more mindful in the future.

- You can list out everything you're grateful for. You could do this randomly, following whatever comes to mind, or you could pick a theme such as your body, or the room you're in. If you want to dig deeper, you could also include a reason why you're grateful for each item – *I'm grateful for the internet because it enables me to connect with people all over the world.*

- Explore your experience with a mindfulness exercise. Maybe you did a meditation. Which one and how did it work for you? Are you able to stay focused or does your mind wander? What kinds of thoughts did you have?

- Do a written mindfulness exercise. You could use the five senses exercise to work through each of your senses and describe what you get from each one. Or you might like to pick an object and describe it in great detail using each of your five senses. For example, you might choose a piece of fruit. Write about how it looks and how you react to its appearance. Pick it up and examine it from all angles. Smell the fruit and describe the scent and whether you have any reactions to it, like your mouth watering. Hold the fruit up to your ear and see if you can make any sound, e.g., by tapping it or unpeeling it (if it has a peel). How does it feel in your hand? Does it weigh much? What's the texture like? Then, when you've finished examining the fruit, you can finally put it in your mouth and describe the taste and how eating it makes you feel.

If none of these exercises appeals to you, you could use a journal prompt to get you started. You might be facing a problem and are unsure how to solve it. You could write out a sentence representing the ideal solution at the top of the page and then journal about why you think you're not there yet.

Here are some prompts you could use to inspire your journaling:

- I am most happy when…
- I am thankful for…
- I forgive myself for…
- I forgive [name] because…
- If I could change one thing about my life it would be… because…

- If my body could talk to me, it would say…
- The thing I love most about myself is… because…
- I am happiest when…
- I am inspired by…
- I am grateful for my family because…
- When I listened to my intuition … happened.
- I can show myself more self-love by…
- I can do more of what I love by…
- I am ready to let go of…
- I am valuable because…
- I can be more patient by…
- I have improved because…
- When my mind starts to wander, I think about…
- I am worried about…
- I felt… today because…
- My five favorite things about myself are…
- I admire…
- If I could say anything to anyone, I would…
- I am at my most productive when…
- I am at my most creative when…
- The best part about being friends with me is…
- I can quit… by…
- I will stop saying to myself…
- The things that fulfil me are…
- When I was a child, I loved… I can do more of this now by…
- My favorite part of the day is…
- What I love most about my home is…
- I can improve my mindset by…
- The emotion that defined today was…
- I can express how I feel by…

- If I could change one thing about today, it would be...
- The song that would describe my mood today would be...
- I can feel less stressed by...
- I can push myself outside my comfort zone by...
- I self-sabotage when I...
- The best part of my day was...
- I am successful because...
- I'm not honest with myself about...
- The biggest lesson from today was...
- If I could redo a conversation or situation from today, I would...
- I feel empowered when...
- Right now, I feel...
- I need more...
- I thought I could never...
- I feel guilty about...
- I moved closer to my goals today by...

Mindful meditation with journaling

You can combine journaling with meditation for an incredibly profound experience. This will take around 15 minutes, so make sure you're not going to be interrupted.

Go somewhere you won't be interrupted. Take a pen and paper with you.

Set a timer for five minutes. Begin this exercise by inhaling deeply, holding the breath for a moment, and then letting it go, sending away any intrusive thoughts with the breath.

Now start writing whatever comes up. It doesn't matter whether these thoughts are deep and meaningful or a mundane consideration of what you're going to eat for dinner. Switch off your inner critic and let whatever words want to come out flow onto the paper.

If your mind is blank, that's okay. Just write *nothing* or *thinking* over and over until something springs to mind and you can follow that thought. All you're trying to do is let your mind vent with whatever words it chooses. If it has nothing to say in the moment, repeatedly writing one word will help you get back into the zone. The more you practice this exercise, the less and less you'll find you're stuck for something to write. Nobody else ever has to see this, so don't let yourself be held back by fear or shame. If it makes you feel better, you can destroy the paper after you've finished this exercise so you know no one will read it.

When your timer goes off, put it on for another five minutes. Now journal how your body is feeling. Start at the top of your head. Maybe you have a tightness or itching there. Perhaps your hair is in your face as you move down to your forehead. How does that feel? How do your eyes feel? Your ears? Your cheeks? Your mouth? Take as long as you need to describe each part of your body all the way to your toes. If the timer goes off before you get there, that's okay. You can choose to continue moving down or you can end the exercise at whatever point you reached.

When your timer goes off again, put it on for a final five minutes. Turn your attention to your breath and watch as it moves in and out. If a thought comes to mind, write it down, then go back to the breath. You have acknowledged the thought as being important to your mind in that moment, but having written it out, you can put your focus back to where you want it to be – your breath. You'll find that the more you do this exercise, the fewer and fewer thoughts you have to write.

Whatever method you choose, try to be mindful as you journal. Keep your focus on what you're writing. If you find yourself being bothered with intrusive thoughts, you might like to explore them. What are the thoughts about? Why do they have the power to draw your attention away from the moment? What's undermining your mindfulness practice? Any and all detail that seems important enough to you to record will be useful.

As journaling becomes a natural part of your daily routine, you'll find yourself looking forward to this time spent in self-reflection. You'll notice how journaling supports you to be more mindful throughout the day.

Summary

- Journaling is a useful way of tracking your progress and appreciating the impact of mindfulness on your life.
- Two ways that are commonly used in therapeutic processes are expressive writing and gratitude journaling.
- Journaling is a practice that has many mental and physical benefits, even if you don't combine it with mindfulness.
- There are myriad ways to journal. Feel free to experiment and choose the approach that's right for you. You can always change it.
- If you're unsure where to start, you could use a journaling prompt to get going.
- You can combine journaling with meditation to help you dig deeper into what's happening in your mind and track your progress as you're able to focus for longer.

CHAPTER NINE:

MINDFUL EATING

So far, we've explored how mindfulness can help you change the way you think to improve your mental health. But mindfulness can also be used to improve your physical wellbeing as well. If you've found it hard to fit mindfulness into your routine, one of the easiest ways is to start eating mindfully. We all need to eat, so when you turn this into a mindful practice, you can bring a mindful aspect into this essential experience. What's more, mindful eating has many positive side effects. It can support you in your weight loss goals, help prevent binging, and nurture a healthier relationship with food[1].

As the name would suggest, mindful eating involves being mindful about what you consume and how. When you eat mindfully, you focus on every aspect of the process, from the first initial craving for food to the physical cues associated with hunger to the experience of eating. In a nutshell, mindful eating means you:

- Slow down when you eat so you can be fully present with every part of the experience without allowing yourself to be distracted.

- Listen to your body's needs so you only eat when you're hungry and stop eating when you've had enough, even if you still have food on your plate.
- Recognize the difference between when you're actually hungry and when your food cravings have another source.
- Immerse yourself fully into the experience, using all your senses to enjoy a multisensory meal. You look at your food before you eat it, appreciate the aroma, observe the texture and flavor so you are conscious on all the effects it has on you.
- Release any negative emotions associated with food, such as guilt or anxiety.
- Treat food as what it is – fuel for your body. You use food as a tool to maintain the health of your body and mind.
- Understand how food impacts your emotions and physical appearance.
- Feel grateful for every bite.

Mindfulness enables you to connect with your body so you can listen to what it's telling you. You can enjoy your food more because you're in tune with yourself throughout the meal. Modern living encourages us to cram as many different things into every second as we can. We multitask when we eat, watching TV, browsing social media, or checking our emails while we aimlessly cram food into our mouths. Eating becomes just another task to complete as quickly as possible so we can tick off more items on our to do list.

Mindful eating empowers us to step away from the array of readily available convenience foods and instead make healthier, more nutritious choices. It transforms a meal into a profound, meaningful experience.

It can take up to 20 minutes or even longer for the brain to notice that you're full[2]. If you're shoveling food in your mouth as fast as you can or distracted by trying to do something else during a meal, it's easy to fall into unhealthy habits because you're not giving your body time to function the way it should. If you eat too fast, your brain may not be able to acknowledge that you're full before you've started overeating. Even if you're not trying to lose weight, overeating has a number of negative side effects that can harm your body. Aside from the obvious risk of obesity, it can also make it harder for you to know if you're really hungry or simply craving comfort food. It can increase your risk of disease such as diabetes or stroke. It may affect your cognitive functioning, which can impact your memory and reasoning[3].

If you want to stay healthy, mindful eating is a simple way of encouraging healthy eating habits.

As with all mindful practices, when you eat mindfully, you're fully focused on what you're doing. This will naturally slow down the process. Every bite is taken with intention rather than being automated. We return to that ability we had as a child. If you observe children, they know how to listen to their bodies. When they're entering into a growth spurt, they can't eat enough. Then, when they need less energy, their appetite wanes. So many parents worry when their child goes through a phase of not eating that they make them ignore the lack of appetite to get something in their stomach. Other times, parents don't want their children to waste food, so they're made to eat everything on their plate, regardless of whether they want it or not. This gradually causes the child to lose that innate ability to follow their body's instincts, which is why we need to reconnect with our body's cues as adults.

Mindful eating helps you to learn how to listen to your body and understand why you get cravings even when you're not hungry.

When you become aware of your triggers, you can detach yourself from them and consciously decide how you want to respond instead of being ruled by them. You can then choose if you still want to eat, but this is your choice rather than an instinctive response to habits that may not be serving you.

Using mindful eating to lose weight

It is widely recognized that diets don't work for most people[4]. While you may find yourself losing weight while following a calorie-controlled diet, the moment you stop monitoring your calories, that weight comes right back again and you end up where you started, if not even heavier. There's a myriad of reasons for this, including genetics, levels of physical exercise, sleep quality, emotional eating, cravings, and stress-causing comfort eating.

A more effective way of losing weight is to change your relationship with food and how you eat, and this is exactly what mindful eating can do[5]. In one study, a six-week program took a group of people with obesity and taught them mindful eating methods. On average, participants lost nine pounds over the course and by the 12-week follow up. Another program supported participants to lose an average of 26 pounds. This weight loss had been maintained when they checked in at the 12-week mark.

Mindfulness can change how you relate to food, altering how you think about it and taking any negative associations and replacing them with awareness, self-control, and more positive thoughts. It can help you deal with the underlying reasons why you consume a poor diet, which then increases your chance of losing weight and maintaining your target weight in the long term.

If you have an issue with binge eating, mindfulness can help you tackle it. This is when you consume vast quantities of food over a short period of time without thinking about the consequences or attempting to stop yourself. Binge eating has been associated with eating disorders and obesity, as well as a higher rate of mental health problems[6]. There is evidence to suggest that when you take a mindfulness approach to eating, it can help combat binge eating[7]. It can also help with emotional eating (when you eat to deal with certain emotions) and negative eating habits, such as when the smell or sight of food leads you to eat, even though you're not hungry[8].

Simple ways to start mindful eating

As you'll discover in a moment, mindful eating can be very involved. If you want to establish new, healthier eating habits, start small and build upon your practice as you adjust to this new way of approaching food. Choose one meal a day for you to practice mindfulness. This might be breakfast as part of your early morning routine where you take time to yourself. It might be lunchtime where you use it as a reason to take a break from the office and have some time to yourself. It might be dinner as a treat to yourself after a long day. As mindful eating becomes second nature to you, you can incorporate it in your other meals.

Here are some ways you can start being more mindful with food:

- **Start the process before you even eat.** When you're shopping, pay close attention to the foods you buy. Look at where they were sourced and consider how they came from there to the shelf. Examine the ingredients to become more conscious about what you're putting in your body. Eat before you go to the store to minimize the chances of choosing items because you're hungry so you impulse-buy comfort foods.

- **Decide whether you're really hungry.** Before you eat anything, check in with yourself to see if you're actually hungry or if there's another reason behind your wanting to eat. You can also take this moment to ask yourself whether you're making a healthy choice with your food. It's okay if you're not. This isn't about beating yourself up or feeling guilty about choosing unprocessed or unhealthy foods. But make sure your choices are coming from a place of power rather than because it's what you've always eaten and you don't want to change your habits, or if it's just to satisfy a craving.
- **Choose meals that involve active preparation.** Rather than shoving a ready meal in the microwave, take time to prepare your food from scratch. There are plenty of nutritious meals you can make that don't have to be complicated or involved. You could make a salad for yourself with a home-made dressing. You can whip up a delicious soup in fifteen minutes.

  When you cook your own food, you automatically have a connection with it. You can extend your mindfulness practice to include preparation. Be mindful about the ingredients you select, the way you prepare them, and how focused you are as you cook.

  If you're new to cooking your own food, don't be too ambitious. You could put together a packed lunch the night before with a sandwich, fruit, and salad. Or do a Google search for quick and simple recipes and follow a step-by-step YouTube video to make your dinner.

  As you get into cooking your own food, you'll discover just how satisfying it is to eat something you've poured your energy into. As you gain confidence in your culinary skills, you can start experimenting with new tastes and textures.

- **Instead of snacking, eat properly.** We often find ourselves grazing on snacks in between meals. This is a quick and easy way to lose track of how much you're really eating. You might find it helpful to plan meals in advance to avoid snacking. If you do find yourself wanting to snack because it has become a habit, be more mindful in your choice of snack. Alternatively, you could divide your meals up throughout the day with smaller portions. Have set mealtimes that fit in with your routine and consider whether you're getting a nutritionally balanced diet.

- **Eat slowly.** For so many of us, a meal is something to be rushed through so we can get on to allegedly more important things. Slow things down to savor your food. Chew thoroughly so you can focus on the sensations of eating and support your digestion.

- **Eliminate distractions.** While giving yourself as much time as it takes to eat consciously and carefully, avoid any distractions so you can be completely in the moment. Switch off the TV. Put the books to one side. Forget about the newspaper. Stop scrolling through social media. Keep your attention on your food and nothing else.

- **Try eating in a different room.** It may be that you've developed the habit of eating at your desk or in front of the TV. With the best will in the world, you may still find yourself falling into your old ways because it's a natural response. You can support yourself to break these old patterns of behavior by eating somewhere new. This will help you be more mindful with your meals because this new place will be associated with the act of eating and nothing else.

- **Don't talk while you're eat.** You may have been told that it's rude to eat with your mouth full, but you can take this a step further by not talking at all while you're eating. If you're sitting down for a meal with family or friends, ask if it's okay to leave conversations until you've finished eating. While you might enjoy talking about your day with the people around you, it's impossible to be fully focused if you're talking and eating. You cannot be mindful about more than one thing at the same time. It might feel weird at first, but you may well all find you enjoy your food a whole lot more if you stay quiet until you're done. If this really isn't possible, see if you can at least be silent for a few minutes.
- **Pay attention to how you feel while you're eating.** Do you get an emotional reaction to your food? How are you feeling while you eat? Does the food bring out any particular feelings in you? How is your body reacting to it? Examine the impact of the food on every level of your being. What is the texture of the food? How does it taste? Think about every part of the experience.
- **Stop eating when you're full.** It doesn't matter if you still have food on your plate. It doesn't matter if there's only one mouthful left. Stop when you feel full. When you eat more slowly and intentionally, your body will have the opportunity to recognize the signals that tell it when you're full. As you become more mindful with your meals, you may well find you need to serve yourself smaller portions because your needs are being met with less food. As you adjust to your new way of eating, you can then change how much food you prepare, reducing the portions in accordance with how hungry you are.

- **Take a moment to remember what you ate yesterday.** This could be an exercise you do in your journal at the end of the day. But ask yourself right now what you ate yesterday. Chances are you probably can't remember because the food wasn't all that important to you. You were eating because that's what your body demanded but you didn't care about the food itself. As you become more intentional about your meals, you can reflect on what you ate the day before to help you plan what you might want to eat today. You may have noticed that some foods have a positive effect on your body and mood while others cause negative side effects. This process could help you identify intolerances and foods that are better for you to avoid because of how they make you feel.

Mindful eating meditation

If you like, you can incorporate meditation with every meal. This can transform eating into a spiritual experience and help you discover the wonder in life, even though eating is a chore you have to do every day to fuel your body.

If you want to meditate with your food, decide on the food and/or drink you want to mindfully consume. Go somewhere quiet where you can focus on your food without any interruptions. You don't want to have to talk to anyone or break your focus during your meditation.

Make yourself comfortable and close your eyes. Bring your focus to your breath. Watch how it flows in and out of your body. Let your breath ease any stress or tension, allowing yourself to relax with every inhale and exhale.

As you relax into your meditation, start scanning your body. Notice the current physical sensations. Pay attention to how your body is resting against a chair and where it's in contact with it. Feel any areas of stress or tension and let the breath make you feel calmer and more peaceful. If any thoughts or emotions come up, acknowledge them and then breathe them away without judgment. Let yourself go into that beautiful place of quiet stillness, that place of being present in the now so you can be completely in the moment.

In your own time, notice where you feel hungry or thirsty in your body. What is that sensation like for you? As you do this scan, you might find that you're not feeling hungry or thirsty at all, and that's okay. Sit with those sensations and accept them for what they are.

Ask yourself, if you could eat or drink anything right now, what would you choose? What is your body telling you it needs? What is the best way to satiate your hunger? What would slake your thirst? Tune into your body's needs and observe how you feel as you think about what you really want in this moment.

Open your eyes and look at the food you've selected. It may be completely different to the foods you just identified and that's fine. This is information you can use next time you eat.

Gaze at the food in front of you as if you've never seen it before. What color is it? What shape is it? How big is it? Is the appearance appealing to you or are you indifferent? What do you think the texture will be like? Turn the plate around so you can look at the food from all angles and make note of your response to the food and the conclusions you're instinctively making about it.

Now imagine all the things that had to take place for your food to be on this plate in front of you right now. Maybe it started as a seed planted in a field somewhere. A farmer took the time to nurture that seed with fertilizer. The sun shone down on it. The rain watered it. As it grew to maturity and was harvested, someone had to arrange for it to be transported to the place where you purchased it. Think about all the work that went into gathering the food, packaging it, processing it, and making it ready for you.

If you're eating something you grew in your garden or maybe some bread or cake you made yourself, this is even better. You can take some time to think about all the love you put into the food as it developed.

You might find it helpful to spend some time feeling grateful for all the people you'll never know who played a part in getting this food and drink on the table in front of you.

When you're ready, pick up the food and consider how it feels in your hand. How would you describe the texture? Is it hot or cold? Is it sticky or wet? Think about how you're responding to the food without judgment or criticism. Let your experience be your experience as you maintain your focus on the food.

Once you've explored how it feels, bring the food up to your nose so you can notice the aroma. Inhale deeply and connect to its scent. Does it inspire any memories in you? How does your body react to the smell? Is your mouth watering? Are you smiling in anticipation? Smell is one of the most important senses when it comes to savoring your food, so give your nose a full opportunity to enjoy the food.

When you feel the time is right, put the food in your mouth, being aware of how your arm and hand move to get the food in your mouth. Let it sit in your mouth for a moment without attempting to chew or swallow. Just let it be until you're ready to roll it around your tongue. What does it taste like? Sweet or salty? Savory or bitter? What's the texture like in your mouth? Are you getting any physical responses to it? Are you producing more saliva? Is your stomach rumbling?

Continue to breathe and be relaxed as you appreciate the sensation of this food in your mouth.

Once you have fully explored these feelings, you can bite into the morsel. How does this change the flavor and texture? Chew slowly and consider the different parts of your mouth that are moving as you bite down on the food. How does your jaw move? What's your tongue doing? How's the food moving around your teeth? Continue to observe how the textures, flavors, and feelings change as you chew.

At last, swallow the food. Notice what happens as it moves from your mouth into your throat and then further down. Are there any traces of the food in your mouth after you've swallowed? You might like to close your eyes as you connect with your body and how it feels during this process. How has being this mindful affected your relationship with food? How are you feeling? Do you feel any different to how you were when you began the meditation?

You can continue this meditation with a different type of food. This time, you might like to change how you eat, following your body's instincts to do whatever feels right. Be aware of the choice you've made. How has this changed the experience of eating? What stayed the same? What did you do that was different?

This can be a really intense experience and you may not feel like you want to do it with every meal (or you may simply not be in a position to do this all the time). But if you only follow this process for one meal a week, you will still build a much closer bond with your eating habits.

While you might not want to meditate at every meal, it's a good idea to slow down when you eat so you can completely enjoy the flavors, textures, and sensations associated with your food. You could be mindful while you shop. Look at the origins of your food. Think about how far it's traveled to get to the store. Consider whether it's something you want on your plate or whether you're buying it because of a craving.

For most of us, eating is forgettable. This explains why some of us can't understand why we're not losing weight when we're being 'good' about what we eat. In reality, we're eating more than we recognize. We've just forgotten how much we've consumed because eating is a secondary thought. Our focus is on something we believe is more important while we're eating. You could be eating while you're traveling from one place to another. You could be eating while you're working because you want to finish that project. You could be eating because you have a child doing a class and you need a way to pass the time. You could be eating because you're watching TV or a movie and you're mindlessly snacking to keep your hands occupied. There's an array of activities we get caught up in while we're eating that take our attention away from the moment. Food becomes a habit, not even important because it's fuel for the body. It's yet another activity to cram into the day. We have no idea whether we're eating enough or eating too much because it's not a priority to care.

- Once we've fallen into the habit of multitasking while eating, we start to connect those other activities with food. So, when we're doing something like watching TV or working, our body generates those signals that tell you that you need to eat even though you don't really. In order to meet those demands, we keep food in our bags or stash snacks in drawers so we can eat whenever we want. We've always got easy access to vending machines, fridges, or cupboards filled with convenience food so we can eat whenever we feel a craving. We kid ourselves that those snacks fill a hole inside us because they give us that feeling of comfort when they're just papering over the cracks. What we really need is to reexamine our priorities and decide what truly matters to us.

When you start mindful eating, you'll discover just how profound and transformational it can be. It can change your life – and your waistline! When you consciously make the effort to be mindful with this most fundamental of activities, you can elevate your relationship with food to a new level. You automatically build different habits. You give yourself a break from the stress of daily life because you're stepping back from the world around you so you can appreciate your food.

Eating mindfully encourages you to make better choices about your diet without your having to make any extra effort. We already know which foods are healthy and which ones aren't so good for us. Eating mindfully doesn't mean you have to give up your mid-morning chocolate bar or stop drinking soda. But when you start making active choices about what you put in your body, these become a savored treat on top of a balanced diet rather than your main source of energy.

Summary

- Mindful eating is an easy way of being more mindful in your daily routine.
- Mindful eating involves focusing on the entire process of eating from the moment you first start feeling like you want to eat something right the way through to chewing and swallowing.
- Mindful eating encourages you to slow down and be present. You learn to listen to your body's cues to understand when you're hungry and when you're craving food for a different reason.
- Mindful eating engages all the senses so you can fully appreciate your food.

- Mindful eating helps you develop healthier eating habits and build a better relationship with food.
- Mindful eating can support you if you want to lose weight by making you more conscious about your eating patterns and supporting you to change your habits for long-lasting, positive change.
- You might like to start being more mindful with just one meal before expanding the practice to every time you eat.
- Start your mindful eating in the store while you're selecting the foods you want to buy.
- Before you eat anything, ask yourself whether you're really hungry or if there's another reason you want to turn to food.
- Cook meals that require active preparation rather than conveniently ready meals.
- Eat proper meals instead of snacking.
- Slow down when you eat so you can be fully present.
- Cut out distractions so you can give all your attention to your food.
- If you find it hard to be mindful when you eat, try eating in a different room.
- Don't talk while you eat – this counts as multitasking!
- As you eat, notice how you're feeling, both physically and emotionally.
- Stop eating when you're full, even if you've still got food left.
- Make a concerted effort to remember what you ate yesterday.
- Meditate while you eat. Really think about every step of the process, from the journey your food took to get onto your plate to how it looks, smells, and feels.

CHAPTER TEN:

MINDFULNESS MEDITATION

Many people conflate mindfulness with meditation. As you will have seen, you don't need to meditate at all to be mindful. That's why I've left meditation to such a late chapter. By now, if you're feeling any hesitancy about trying meditation, you can be reassured that you can live a mindful life without it.

However, if you don't at least try meditation, you'll be denying yourself what can be a profound, life changing experience with many benefits. Mindfulness does not mean meditating, but most meditations are mindful. During a meditation, you are keeping your focus on a point of your choosing without letting your mind wander. When you do a specifically mindful meditation, it can help you be more mindful elsewhere in your life.

There is a wealth of evidence supporting the benefits of meditation. It can:

- Lower stress
- Lower anxiety levels
- Improve your self-image
- Give you a more positive outlook

- Increase self-awareness
- Build up your attention span
- Counter age-related memory loss
- Make you kinder
- Improve your quality of sleep
- Help you deal with pain
- Lower blood pressure[1]

If you're looking to mindfulness to improve your life, adding meditation into your routine will help you see the difference sooner. Daily meditation can help you identify how your thoughts can affect your emotions, even when you're trying to control them. It also supports you to identify the types of behavior that bring positive outcomes so you can practice them more and let those habits that aren't so healthy fall away.

Maybe you've tried to meditate before and felt that it was impossible for you. Maybe you struggled to sit still or couldn't empty your mind. The reality is that meditation is not asking your mind to do anything it wouldn't naturally do. When we meditate, our mind experiences alpha and theta waves. These are the same type of brain waves you have when you're relaxed or asleep[2]. All you are doing is intentionally inducing this relaxed state. But when you first start meditating, it's a new experience. Your mind isn't used to you telling it what to think. It fights against the process, which is why you'll find your mind wandering. This is absolutely normal. Meditation isn't about emptying the mind. Your mind is designed to think, and trying to get it to stop its natural function is next to impossible. Instead, it's about controlling what your mind thinks about. You are understanding your mind's unique patterns to understand and control your thought processes.

There are as many different types of meditation as there are meditators. So, if you've struggled to get into meditation, it's highly likely you haven't found the right meditation for your way of thinking. It's pointless trying to do a guided visualization if you're one of those people who isn't a visual thinker. Alpha personality types often struggle with the passive forms of meditation like watching the breath but do well with chanting, mantras, or even moving meditations.

That's why I'm going to give you a range of meditation techniques so you can explore the various approaches to discover which ones you enjoy, and those that don't resonate. Try a technique for a few days before deciding it's not for you. It takes a while to master any new skill, and meditation is no different. You can use your journal to see if it's getting easier or whether you might want to try a different method.

Whatever type of meditation you pick, don't get frustrated with yourself if you find your attention drifting or you're getting intrusive thoughts. Just pull your mind back to your chosen focus. You might like to acknowledge the thought with a *thank you* and tell it you'll come back to it later. You could imagine tying the thought to a balloon string and let it float away. Or you could think of it as a fallen leaf dropping onto a river and being carried away by the water. You'll find that the longer you maintain a meditation habit, the easier it becomes to stay focused and the fewer interruptions you have.

Set yourself up for success with your meditation practice. Start small. Meditating for just a couple of minutes every day will still have positive benefits and it's better to meditate for two minutes without losing your focus than trying to do 20 minutes and finding that all you can think about is how much longer you've got to sit still. It will be more beneficial if you meditate for a couple of minutes every day than trying to do an hour once a month. You can then gradually extend the amount of time you're meditating because you're building on a regular practice and working with your mind rather than jumping in at the deep end[3].

Here are some of the most popular forms of mindfulness meditation. You'll find that we've touched upon some of these techniques earlier in the book. If you've been implementing these suggestions, you may have discovered that they're much simpler than you thought, and you can use that as the foundation of your meditation practice.

Breathwork

Working with the breath is one of the simplest forms of meditation. While it's straightforward, it's deceptively powerful and always available to you. We've already covered a number of breathing techniques you can use to be more mindful. Here are some other ways you can use your breath to meditate. With each technique, make yourself comfortable with your back straight and supported. You want to allow the breath to flow freely without restriction. It's better to sit up while you're meditating so you're less likely to fall asleep. Set a timer before you start and breathe until it goes off. Try starting with just two minutes and gradually increase the amount of time until you can meditate for 20 minutes or more.

A word of caution: Some breathing meditations involve controlling the breath and this may not be appropriate for you if you have issues with your breathing. If you find that you get uncomfortable in any way while you're doing a breathwork meditation, stop and try a different method. If you have any concerns, consult a medical professional to see if breathwork is right for you.

1. **Abdominal breathing**

   Put your right hand on your chest and your left hand on your belly.

   Inhale deeply through your nose and observe how the intake of air makes your hands move.

Exhale slowly through your mouth and watch how your hands return to their original position.

Repeat until the timer goes off.

2. **Equal breathing**

Choose a number that suits your breathing rhythm. Four is usually a good one to start.

Slowly inhale through your nose, counting to four in your mind.

Slowly exhale through your nose, counting to four in your mind.

Repeat until the timer goes off.

3. **Counting breaths**

There are a couple of variations with this meditation. You can count on the inhale or count on the exhale. You can repeat the same number on inhale and exhale, i.e., one, one, two, two, three, three, etc. You can count one on the inhale, two on the exhale, three on the inhale, four on the exhale, and so on.

Whatever option you choose, count your breaths up to ten, then go back to one and begin again. If you lose count or find you've counted higher than ten, that's okay. Simply return to one and start over.

4. **Counting forward and backward**

This is another twist on counting the breaths. Choose a number (four or ten are good) and count up to that with the breath and then count back down again. For example:

Inhale and count one.

Exhale.

Inhale and count two.

Exhale.

Inhale and count three.

Exhale.

Inhale and count four.

Exhale.

Inhale and count three.

Exhale.

Inhale and count two.

Exhale.

Inhale and count one.

Repeat this until the timer goes off.

5. Alternate nostril breathing

This is a more advanced technique that can take a while to master but is well worth mastering. It involves closing and opening alternate nostrils with your thumb and ring finger. You might find it helpful to rest your first and middle finger against the space between your eyebrows while you do this.

Close your right nostril with your right thumb.

Inhale deeply through your left nostril.

Move your thumb so the right nostril is open and close your left nostril with your right ring finger.

Exhale slowly through your right nostril.

Inhale deeply through your right nostril.

Move your ring finger so your left nostril is open and close your right nostril with your thumb.

Exhale slowly through your left nostril.

Repeat until your timer goes off and then make sure you finish your practice with an exhale on the left side.

6. Rhythmic breathing

This form of counting the breaths involve following a regular pattern. Depending on how fast or slow your breath, you can follow a 4-2-4-2 pattern, a 6-3-6-3 pattern, or even an 8-4-8-4 pattern. You may find that as you meditate, your breathing slows so you might like to extend the count to a longer one. The most important thing is that you're holding your breath for half of the inhale and exhale count.

If you're using a 4-2-4-2 pattern, it would look like this:

Inhale as you count to four in your mind.
Hold your breath while you count to two.
Exhale as you count to four in your mind.
Hold your breath while you count to two.
Repeat until your timer goes off.

Body scan meditation

I've mentioned scanning your body a few times in this book. This is a longer version of that process that takes around 20 minutes to do, compared to spending a minute or two checking in with how you're physically feeling. It's a good idea to do this multiple times a week so you can familiarize yourself with how your body normally feels and track any changes to build a deeper understanding of yourself and your body.

You can do this meditation sitting up or lying down. You might like to do it last thing at night to relax before you go to sleep. It's also a good practice to do first thing in the morning so you can be mindful from the moment you wake up.

Go somewhere you won't be disturbed and make yourself comfortable. Close your eyes and turn your attention to your breath. Inhale deeply and exhale three times to ground and center yourself into your body.

Become aware of your body's weight. Notice where your body is in contact with the chair, bed, cushion, or floor and watch it becoming heavier, sinking down into relaxation.

Tune into your breath. As you inhale, became aware of the oxygen flowing into your body. Feel gratitude for this simple way of nurturing yourself. With each exhale, breathe away any stress or tension and with each inhalation, bring in more and more gratitude. Do this for a few cycles of breath, allowing yourself to relax further with each breath.

When you are ready, bring your focus to your feet. Notice where they're touching the floor. Consider how this feels. Think about how your feet support your weight and transport you around. Feel thankful for your feet and all they do for you.

When you're ready, gently bring your awareness higher to your legs. How relaxed do they feel? Are they resting against anything like a chair or a bed? How does it feel? What part of your legs are in contact and how does that feel? Allow yourself to be grateful for your legs and all they do for you.

When you're ready, bring your focus higher still to your back. Is it straight? Is it supported? Do you notice any tension or pain in your back? Breathe away any stress and feel thankful for your back and how it supports you all the time.

When you're ready, bring your attention round to the front and your stomach area. Notice how it rises and falls with every breath, this gentle movement constantly reminding you that you're alive. If you see any stress or tension here, use the breath to send it away. Feel thankful for your abdomen and all it does for you.

When you're ready, gently take your focus higher to your heart and chest. Is your breath making this area move? Is it calm and relaxed or are you carrying tension in your chest? Let your breath relax you more and more. Feel thankful for your heart and how it continues to keep energy flowing throughout your body.

When you're ready, take a moment to check in with your hands. How are they feeling? Are they relaxed or stiff? Ask them to relax even further and as they loosen, feel thankful for your hands and everything they do for you every day.

When you're ready, bring your awareness higher to examine your arms. How are they feeling? Are they resting against something? What does that feel like? Are you holding any stress or tension here? Breathe it away. Feel thankful for your arms and all they do for you.

When you're ready, move your focus up to your neck and throat. Are they open and allowing the breath to flow? Can they be even more relaxed? Is your jaw loose or do you need to relax it further? Feel thankful for everything your neck and throat does for you.

When you're ready, observe your whole head. Is your facial expression soft and calm? Do you feel relaxed or is there tension somewhere, say, your scalp? Feel thankful for everything your head does for you.

Once you have finished scanning your body, do another quick scan of it as a whole being. Could you be even more relaxed? Does any part need you to send more breath to help it unwind?

When you're ready, inhale and exhale deeply, letting the breath flow to all parts of your body. Stretch, yawn, feeling yourself coming out of the meditation. When you are ready, open your eyes.

Moving meditation

If you find it difficult to sit in stillness, you can ease your way into meditation with mindful movement. This involves connecting with your body and being fully present with its movements. Lots of people find that when their body is engaged, it's easier to quiet the mind because they're fully focused on the doing and don't need to think about anything else.

There are many different types of mindful movement, including yoga, t'ai chi, and qi gong. You could look for a local class to learn more about these powerful meditations. If you can't get to a class in person, there are lots of videos available online you can follow. Dance can also be a type of meditation. Let your inner child lead the way as you put on music with a catchy beat and let your body move without worrying about how coordinated you are or whether your moves look good.

We've gone into a few types of walking meditation in this book. If you don't enjoy those techniques, another variation is to do a walking meditation in water. Go to your local pool or beach and watch your body as you slowly walk through the water. You could keep your focus on your feet, or you could observe your hands as you move. Water changes how the light hits your body so this will give you a different perspective, which can be fascinating. You might find that walking in water is an easy way to tap into a meditative state because it's so different from how you normally walk.

Labeling your thoughts

Sometimes people stress because they keep getting intrusive thoughts while they try to meditate. This stress stops them from immersing themselves in the meditative state far more than any extraneous thoughts do, but it becomes almost impossible to let them go.

Rather than trying to stop these thoughts, you can make them work for you in your meditation.

Set a timer for as long as you'd like to meditate. You could start with five minutes and gradually extend the length of your meditation.

Sit quietly and inhale deeply and exhale to settle yourself in the moment. Wait for a thought to come up without forcing it. When it does, don't follow the thought or start to consider it. Instead, label it according to the type of thought it is (Plan? Stress? Insight?) and whether it's about the past, present, or future.

Once you've labeled it, let it go and wait for another thought. If the same thought comes back again, label it again and let it go. Eventually, it will pass.

Do this until your timer goes off.

Guided visualizations

These meditations are a simple way for many people to get into meditating. As I've mentioned earlier, not everyone can visualize so if you can't see things in your mind, you might like to try a different form of meditation. Alternatively, rather than trying to see the scenes described, you could use your other senses to sense what's in front of you or simply 'know' and trust that it's there. Think of it as like being in your home when it's dark and the lights are off. You know where all the furniture is even though you can't see it.

You can write your own script if you have a particular issue you want to address with meditation. You could then memorize it and recreate it in your mind, but most people find it easier to record themselves and listen to the recording so they can be guided through the meditation. Alternatively, there are plenty of guided meditations available for free online, so whatever you want to meditate about, you're bound to find something on the internet.

Alternatively, here are some scripts you can use to enjoy a nice, relaxing meditation:

1. **Giving your worries to the fire**
   Sit comfortably and close your eyes. Turn your attention to your breath. Watch it flow in and out without trying to control or change it in any way.

As you focus on your breath, you notice that the sound of your breath is changing, becoming the crackling of a fire.

You realize that you're sitting by a campfire. The flames warm you and give off a comforting light.

You sit comfortably by the fire, allowing the flames to soothe you. Take a moment to watch them flicker and burn, enjoying this moment of stillness and peace. This time is just for you, and you can take as long as you want to appreciate the beauty of the fire.

You become aware of a pen and paper lying on the ground next to you. You pick it up and realize that this is your opportunity to free yourself from anything that's been worrying you.

You start writing, detailing all the things that have been bothering you. You have as much paper as you need to write about all your worries. Let anything that's causing you stress flow out and onto the page.

When you've finished writing, fold the paper in half and then half again. Hold it to your heart for a moment, filling it with love. All these worries have taught you a lesson, but you no longer need them in your life and it's time to let them go with love.

Toss the paper into the flames and watch it burn. Maybe you see the flames make shapes and patterns as they consume the paper, sending you a message about how your problems can be resolved.

Know that you can come back to this place any time you like. But for now, it's time to leave. Say goodbye to the fire as you bring your focus back to your body.

You might like to wiggle your fingers, wiggle your toes, yawn, and stretch as you come back into yourself. When you're ready, you can open your eyes and go about the rest of your day.

2. **A relaxing day at the beach**

Make yourself comfortable and close your eyes. Turn your attention to your breath. Observe how it flows in… and out… in… and out…

As you continue to breathe, you realize that the sound of your breath is really the sound of the sea. You are by the ocean, waves gently breaking against the shoreline. You are perfectly safe. There is nothing here that can harm you.

The sun blazes overhead in a perfectly clear blue sky. You can hear the sound of seagulls in the distance, but they're not loud enough to disturb your calm. You are wonderfully and perfectly relaxed.

You can feel the sand beneath your body, warmed by the sun. You grab a handful of sand and let it trickle through your fingers, enjoying the feel of the grains in your hand.

You notice a pebble by you. You pick it up and hold it, loving its smooth texture.

You realize you can fill this pebble with your problems if you need a break from worrying about them.

Hold the pebble in both hands, close your eyes, and send all your troubles into the stone. Feel the stone getting heavier as it takes on all those things that are causing you pain or distress.

When you feel the stone is full, stand up. Throw the stone as far away from you as possible into the sea. Know that the water will take away your problems, so you don't have to worry about them anymore.

Sit back down on the beach and notice how you're feeling much calmer and more relaxed. Feel the sun on your skin, warming you, helping you feel even more rested and relaxed.

This is your place, and you can come back here any time you like, but for now it's time to leave. Take a moment to say goodbye to the sea, thanking it for taking away your fears, doubts, and concerns.

Bring your attention back to your breath and notice how it no longer sounds like the sea. You are returning to your body, coming back to your regular life.

You might like to stretch, tilt your head from side to side, and become more aware of your body.

When you're ready, open your eyes and go about the rest of your day.

Intentional awareness meditation

With an intentional awareness meditation, you bring your awareness to different aspects of your being – usually your breath, body, sounds, thoughts, and feelings, in that order. This is an exercise in accepting the present moment for what it is. You do not decide what's happening at any given time. You just observe and allow.

Make yourself comfortable and close your eyes. Bring your focus to your breath and watch as you breathe in and out. Do not attempt to try to change or control your breath. Just watch the flow of air for a while. If you find your mind straying to other thoughts, gently pull it back to your breath.

When you're ready, turn your attention to your body. You do not need to do a full body scan like in the earlier meditation, but you could decide to follow this process to note any sensations from your head to your toes. Or you may prefer to see what part of your body is calling for your attention. Are you holding any stress or tension in a particular area? Let it relax. Become aware of any physical sensations, such as where your body is in contact with a chair or the ground. Continue to watch and allow any tension to melt away.

Once you feel that you are completely conscious of your body and its present state, turn your attention to your hearing. What noises can you hear? Let these sounds support you to become even more relaxed. If you can't make out any sounds, tune into the silence instead. How does it feel to sit in the absence of sound?

After a few minutes of exploring the sounds you can hear, turn your awareness to whatever thoughts may come forward. Let thoughts float through your mind without judging them or attempting to control them. Become a thoughtful observer, understanding that you are not your thoughts. They are separate to your inner being. They do not have to be associated with any value judgment or emotion.

Take your attention away from your thoughts and turn to your emotions instead. Let yourself feel however you want to feel in this moment. Notice whether these emotions affect any specific parts of your body. Watch your emotions as you recognize that they are not you. You can choose whether to be controlled by your emotions or whether you feel a certain way.

Finally, let your focus be taken by whatever is most demanding your attention. This could be your body, your thoughts, your breath, the sounds around you, or your emotions. Whatever seems to be most important at this time, let that fill your awareness.

When you're ready, inhale deeply, hold it for a moment, and then release. You may now open your eyes.

Loving kindness or Metta meditation

Loving kindness or Metta meditation comes from a Buddhist practice. When carried out regularly, it confers all the benefits of regular meditation, as well as increasing your levels of compassion, kindness, and empathy[4]. You always start by sending yourself love before sending it to others, starting with those you are closest to and expanding out to people you don't know as well – even those you don't like or are currently having issues with.

When you first start doing loving kindness meditations, you might prefer to start small and simply send love to yourself and your loved ones. It can be difficult to accept love for yourself if you're not used to doing this, so lay the foundations of your practice by starting with yourself and one other person and then gradually expand as you feel ready. Likewise, it can be hard to send love to someone you don't like right now, so if you don't feel ready to do that, skip that part of the meditation for now.

Sit comfortably with your back supported. Close your eyes and turn your attention to your breath. Let it take you into a relaxed state of calm.

When you feel ready, open your heart to feeling love. Let it fill your heart and then spread out to the whole of your being. Understand that you are perfect just as you are. You are worthy of love. It is okay to make mistakes. You still deserve love.

With every inhalation, pull in more love and allow yourself to sink into this wonderful feeling of being loved.

When you feel ready, say to yourself, *May I be happy. May I feel love. May I always be at peace. May I be happy. May I feel love. May I always be at peace. May I be happy. May I feel love. May I always be at peace.*

Sit for a moment, allowing yourself to bask in this love.

When you're ready, think of someone you love, someone you're close to, someone you're grateful to have in your life. Send love to that person, saying to yourself, *May they be happy. May they feel love. May they always be at peace. May they be happy. May they feel love. May they always be at peace. May they be happy. May they feel love. May they always be at peace.*

Now think of someone you don't know as well. Maybe it's a neighbor whose name you don't know. Maybe it's a sales assistant who regularly serves you at the store. Maybe it's someone you see on your commute but don't speak to. Send them love as you say to yourself, *May they be happy. May they feel love. May they always be at peace. May they be happy. May they feel love. May they always be at peace. May they be happy. May they feel love. May they always be at peace.*

Now think about someone you are currently in conflict with, someone with whom you have a difficult relationship. Send them love too, saying to yourself, *May they be happy. May they feel love. May they always be at peace. May they be happy. May they feel love. May they always be at peace. May they be happy. May they feel love. May they always be at peace.*

Sit here for a while, pulling in love with every inhale and sending love with every exhale. Know that someone, somewhere is also doing a loving kindness meditation, sending love to you just as you're sending it to them. Say to yourself, *May we all be happy. May we all feel love. May we all always be at peace. May we all be happy. May we all feel love. May we all always be at peace. May we all be happy. May we all feel love. May we all always be at peace.*

Take as long as you need to sit in this beautiful feeling of being loved. When you are ready, open your eyes and go about the rest of your day.

Summary

- While meditation is a mindful practice, you do not need to meditate to be mindful. Still, you might like to incorporate it into your mindfulness routine because meditation brings with it many benefits and supports you to be more mindful in the rest of your life.
- There are countless different ways to meditate. If you find it hard to connect with one method, try a different one until you discover what works for you.
- Start small and gradually expand your practice as you become more confident in your meditating.
- Breathwork is a popular way of working with your breath. If you have any health issues with your respiratory system, check with your medical professional before you start a breathwork practice.
- Different types of breathwork include abdominal breathing, equal breathing, counting breaths, counting forward and backward, alternate nostril breathing, and rhythmic breathing.
- Body scan meditations involve observing each part of your body in detail, starting at your feet and slowly working your way up. It can be good to do before you go to sleep to relax you or first thing in the morning to be more mindful.
- If you don't like sitting still for long periods, you could try mindful movement. Examples include yoga, t'ai chi, qi gong, dance, or walking in water.
- You do not have to empty your mind when you meditate. You can work with your thoughts, labeling them before letting them leave your mind.
- Guided visualizations involve listening to a script and visu-

alizing the scene in your mind. Not everyone has a visual imagination, so you may prefer to sense or know what's being described is there. There are plenty of examples online or you can write your own script and record it to listen to.

- Intentional awareness meditations involve you focusing on your breath, body, sounds, thoughts, and feelings, and then letting whatever seems most important come to the fore.
- Loving kindness or Metta meditation is the practice of sending love to yourself and then to those around you. You can send love just to your nearest and dearest, or you can build on your practice to send it to strangers, those you don't like, and the whole world.

CHAPTER ELEVEN:

MINDFULNESS APPS

Mindfulness encourages us to be in the moment and breaking our reliance on technology. As such, it might seem strange to recommend apps for mindfulness. However, technology is a part of modern living. When used appropriately, it can support you to develop your mindfulness practice and build better, healthier habits.

There are many alternatives available. This is a brief overview of some of the more popular ones, paid and free, that you can incorporate into your mindfulness practice.

Insight Timer

Insight Timer offers free and paid options to access over 25,000 guided meditations recorded by 3,000 meditation teachers. As you can imagine, there are meditations covering every subject you can imagine, from relationships to work to stress. Whatever you want to meditate about, you're likely to find it in the library here.

Another advantage of Insight Timer is its community. You can see at a glance how many people have meditated that day and how many are meditating at that moment. There are over six million users of the app, so there's always someone to meditate with – the app will even tell you how many other people are doing the meditation with you. If you want to feel like there are people around you sharing your meditation journey, there is a setting to enable you to see who's meditating in your town and what they've chosen to meditate about.

You can follow your favorite teachers to get notifications when they put up new content. There's also a built-in timer with your choice of sounds so you can meditate by yourself for a predetermined amount of time. On top of all of that, you get access to over 2,000 talks and podcasts stuffed full of advice and inspiration. You can end your days with music composed to calm you and send you to sleep.

You could download this app and have everything you need at the touch of a button. However, some people find the number of choices overwhelming and a source of stress rather than something that soothes them. If you're the kind of person who loves lots of options, Insight Timer will be great for you. When you upgrade to the paid version, you'll get extra content, including courses, exclusive daily meditations, and the option to download your favorite meditations so you can listen to them offline and pick them up at any point during the recording.

Ten Percent Happier

Ten Percent Happier is targeted at those people who don't feel like they need to change their life so much as get more out of their current one. It is based around Dan Harris' work. Harris was a news anchor who had a panic attack live on TV. His mental health problems brought him to meditation, and he wrote a book about his experiences and how meditation helped him. Also titled *Ten Percent*

Happier, it's a good read if you want to know more about meditation but are skeptical about whether it will help you.

The app gives you a free course that includes daily videos by Harris for a week, with occasional input from meditation teacher Joseph Goldstein. You also get a daily meditation by Goldstein to help you develop a meditation practice. The week-long course delves into topics like how to know you're really meditating and how you can get over those times when you're finding it hard to get into the zone, making it perfect if you're new to meditation.

If you enjoy the free material, upgrading to the paid version gives you over 350 downloadable meditations and a range of courses on mindfulness, stress, and performance. If you don't want to go to the paid version, you might like to listen to Harris' *Ten Percent Happier* podcast, which has interviews with many leading lights in the mindfulness movement, including the Dalai Lama and Jon Kabat-Zinn.

Smiling Mind

If you want to involve your entire family with your mindfulness practice, Smiling Mind is the app for you. Designed by a team of psychologists, you get a daily meditation that you can customize to the appropriate age group from children ages seven and older, all the way up to adults. In addition, you get access to hundreds of meditations, so you're bound to be able to find one to help with whatever you're going through. The meditations are organized into programs so you can choose the most appropriate beginning point and move between programs as your needs evolve and adapt. Most of the meditations are between 5 and 15 minutes long so can be easily slotted into your day, but if you have more time available, there are some longer 45-minute meditations to try.

Smiling Mind is more than a meditation app. It is specifically designed to help you be more mindful throughout your life, so there are plenty of mindful activities you can use to become more mindful throughout the day. For example, there's an activity to help you develop your active listening skills and turn a conversation into a meditative experience.

Smiling Mind really is a great app and, what's more, it's totally free. There's no option to upgrade to paid status, so there are no ads or content hidden behind a paywall.

UCLA Mindful

UCLA Mindful was put together by the Mindful Awareness Research Center based at the University of California (UCLA). It doesn't have as many meditations as the other apps mentioned in this chapter – only about 12 basic meditations – but the app is completely free with no paid option, so you have access to all the content on the app.

While there may not be many meditations, they cover a range of techniques so you can try them all to find which ones resonate with you. You can experiment with breathwork, facing your emotions, Metta meditation, and more. None of the meditations are too long or involved, so whether you only have a couple of minutes to spare or you can sit down for 20 minutes, you know you'll be able to fit in a meditation.

UCLA Mindful includes a Getting Started section to guide you through the basics if mindfulness is a new experience for you. It gives advice on how to find the right meditation or how to sit while you're meditating, and includes lots of research about the benefits associated with the meditations.

You'll also find podcasts on the app, half-hour recordings of the lunchtime meditations that are offered on the UCLA campus. You can listen to the discussions before and after the meditation and spend time in silent contemplation.

Given UCLA Mindful was created by a respected academic institute, you can feel confident that everything you find on the app has a basis in the science of meditation and is thus trustworthy.

Summary

- While you don't want to rely heavily on technology to be mindful, there are many apps that can be a helpful addition to your mindfulness practice.
- Insight Timer has paid and free options and thousands of meditations for you to choose from. It also has a community, so you don't have to feel alone while you meditate.
- Ten Percent Happier is based on the work of Dan Harris, a news anchor who used meditation to help him deal with his mental health. There's a free week-long course and daily meditations on the app, as well as a podcast. If you upgrade to the paid version, you get access to more than 350 downloadable meditations.
- Smiling Mind is a good app for families. It has meditations suitable for all ages from seven right the way through to adulthood. This app has a stronger focus on mindfulness than some of the other apps.
- UCLA Mindful was designed by the Mindful Awareness Research Center at UCLA. It's a free app with many meditations so you can explore the various techniques, as well as recordings of the lunchtime meditations held on campus.

CHAPTER TWELVE:

MINDFULNESS-BASED COGNITIVE THERAPY (MBCT)

While this isn't the place to dig into MBCT in extensive depth, I feel that it is important to touch upon it if you feel that self-guided mindfulness isn't enough for you to deal with your issues, and you'd like some professional support.

MCBT is a relatively new form of psychotherapy that brings together cognitive behavioral therapy (CBT) and mindfulness techniques to provide long lasting relief from major depressive disorders. It's recommended by the National Institute for Health and Care Excellence (NICE) in the UK as a treatment for those suffering from recurrent depression, as there is evidence to suggest that it lowers the relapse rate by as much as 43%[1]. Not only can it help with depression, research has also found that MBCT can help combat addiction. For example, in one study, smokers who used mindfulness meditation for a fortnight cut their smoking by 60% and had fewer cravings for a cigarette, even if they didn't plan on quitting[2].

MBCT draws upon parts of CBT, including teaching participants about depression and how cognition impacts mood. It utilizes a range of techniques to do this, including 'decentering,' which is a way of being aware of your thoughts and feelings and accepting them without judgment or reaction. This is akin to many mindfulness methods and helps participants to stop and reprogram their automatic responses so they can make better choices in the future to free themselves from the cycle of negative thinking and self-destructive behavior. Instead of trying to prevent these negative thoughts, MBCT puts a focus on your thought process so you can identify when you're going into a downward spiral and decide to do things differently.

How MBCT works

So-called negative emotions such as sadness and depression are normal responses to upsetting or traumatic experiences. Most of us recover from these feelings on our own, but if you've just recovered from a depressive state, such events can be a trigger to push you into a deeper depression. MBCT looks to break this cycle. Rather than pushing you to avoid those negative feelings, it aims to transform your relationship with those emotions using meditation and mindfulness. The thinking behind MBCT is that it gives individuals the tools to change ingrained patterns of behavior by recognizing that they have alternative responses that are just as valid. Through a regular meditation practice, individuals can use these tools whenever they feel their emotions becoming too powerful so they can replace negative thoughts with positive ones.

If you decide to undergo MBCT, you'll be invited to two-hour group therapy sessions once a week over the course of eight weeks, as well as a full day session at some point between weeks five and seven. These sessions are therapist led and will give you a number of meditation techniques and introduce you to the basic principles of cognition, such as the connection between thoughts and feelings. You may also learn more about depression and its causes and how MBCT can help you deal with it. There will be homework for you to do between sessions, such as breathing exercises and mindful meditations.

You should receive CDs or digital recordings to help you build on what you've learned in sessions in the comfort of your own home. When you come back to class, you can discuss your experiences with the other students and support each other through challenges, as well as celebrating your successes.

By the end of the program, you should know how to:

- Understand the way your mind works
- Notice when you're likely to fall into old ways of thinking that send you on a downward slope
- Break free from negative patterns and choose more positive ways of coping
- Find different ways of connecting with yourself and your environment
- Find the joy in the simple things
- Be kind to yourself and not waste energy hoping for a change or trying to do more than you're capable of
- Stop sabotaging yourself
- Accept yourself for who you are and work towards being your best self

What to look for in an MBCT therapist

An MBCT therapist is a professionally qualified mental health therapist who has studied mindfulness-based practices and techniques in a recognized organization such as the UCSD Mindfulness-Based Professional Training Institute in the States or the Oxford Mindfulness Centre in the UK. While it is always ideal to feel a positive connection with your MBCT therapist, this is less important than with other types of therapy because the program is designed to teach you techniques rather than requiring you to talk about your current situation. A good MBCT therapist should be there to facilitate group learning so their thoughts and opinions or your relationship with them shouldn't matter.

Accessmbct.com is a great resource to help you find your nearest qualified professional. Before you sign up for a course, talk about your circumstance with the therapist so you can be sure that MBCT is the best fit for you. You may also like to ask them about their experiences with MBCT and how their clients have been helped by it.

Practicing MBCT by yourself

Although MBCT was designed to follow a specific process laid out in weekly classes, you may not be able to get to a program for a range of reasons. There may not be a therapist in your area, classes may not be at a convenient time for you, or you may simply not be able to afford it. If this is the case for you, it is possible to experience its benefits without the support of a class.

You can get *The Mindful Way Workbook* from Amazon and work through the material by yourself or with a friend or therapist. Written by John Teasdale, Mark Williams and Zindel Segal, the book comes with a CD and MP3 downloads for you to listen to the guided meditations.

The authors wrote another book in consultation with Jon Kabat-Zinn, who played a leading role in establishing mindfulness as a recognized practice with therapeutic benefits. *The Mindful Way through Depression: Freeing Yourself from Chronic Unhappiness* also has an accompany CD with meditations narrated by Kabat-Zinn to make it easy for you to do them.

Summary

- Mindfulness-based Cognitive Therapy (MBCT) combines mindfulness and cognitive behavioral therapy to provide an effective treatment for depression and addiction.
- It follows an eight-week program to teach participants about depression, its effect on the brain, and how you can use mindfulness to change negative thought patterns and behavior.
- When looking for an MBCT therapist, make sure you work with someone who is appropriately qualified.
- If you cannot attend classes for any reason, there are books available so you can work through the material by yourself.

CONCLUSION

Mindfulness is a powerful practice open to anyone. Although many people think you have to meditate to be mindful – and while it is true that meditation can help you become more mindful – it is not the only way you can be more mindful in your daily life.

Mindfulness supports you to develop an ongoing awareness of what is presently happening without judgment. It allows you to accept what is and stay in the moment, free from stress about the future or obsession over the past. Mindfulness is a state of being you can consciously choose to enter into at any time.

It doesn't matter what your age, religious background, or circumstances. Mindfulness can help you become more self-aware and gain control over your life. You accept responsibility for your choices without blame or recriminations. It helps you to show more love towards yourself and take better care of yourself instead of neglecting your needs or beating yourself up for supposed mistakes.

Mindfulness is a practice that has been with us for centuries. In more recent times, there has been a wealth of scientific research into the effects of mindfulness. If you have any doubts over whether or not it will work for you, there's plenty of evidence out there to show that mindfulness really does have a positive impact on your life. Amongst other things, it can:

- Lower stress
- Decrease anxiety
- Improve your physical, emotional, and mental health
- Reduce emotional, instinctive reactions and enable you to make choices from a place of conscious reasoning
- Improve your memory
- Break the pattern of negative thinking and behavior

This book has given you a range of tools you can use to be more mindful in your daily life. It is up to you to decide how you're going to weave it into your routine. It is a highly personalized, customizable practice that you can tailor to your preferences. You don't have to use all the methods outlined in this book to be mindful. Even if you only choose one or two, you'll still find that it has a positive effect, and you can always incorporate more techniques as you become more comfortable and confident in your mindful lifestyle.

Mindfulness can enrich your life in a multitude of ways. The more mindful you can be, the more you'll appreciate everything life has to offer. Your new mindful attitude will affect the people around you in positive ways, so it's not only you who'll enjoy the benefits. Everyone you know will as well and that's a truly beautiful thing.

I wish you much joy on your mindfulness journey.

THANKS FOR READING

I hope that you enjoyed reading this book and that the lessons and practical exercises have been valuable to you.

If you want to check out more from me, I recommend that you read my book, *The Power of Meditation: Simple Practices for Mental Clarity and Relaxation*. As I outlined in the mindfulness meditation chapter, meditation is an excellent way to compliment your mindfulness practices and get even more out of it. If you liked that chapter and want to learn even more about meditation, I recommend that you read this book.

If you liked these books and want to expand on what you've learned, you can also read my books on Stoicism. This powerful philosophy focuses on personal improvement and mental growth and will compliment the book you've just read nicely. You will even find chapters on mindfulness in them as it is a cornerstone of Stoicism.

I recommend starting with my first book, *Stoicism: How to Use Stoic Philosophy to Find Inner Peace and Happiness*. It's a great place to learn about what Stoicism is and how you can use in your daily life.

You can view these books by visiting bouchardpublishing.com/books

Also, be sure to check out my email list where I am constantly adding tons of value. You will also receive my free four-page meditation tracker that you can use to monitor your progress you have made when you sign up.

You can sign up by visiting bouchardpublishing.com/mindfulness

Kindest regards,
Jason Hemlock

REFERENCES

Introduction

[1] https://floatworks.com/journal/the-five-most-fascinating-scientific-studies-on-mindfulness

[2] https://www.psych.ox.ac.uk/research/mindfulness

Chapter One

[1] https://link.springer.com/article/10.1007/s12671-018-1087-9

Chapter Two

[1] https://www.latimes.com/science/sciencenow/la-sci-sn-americans-less-happy-20190323-story.html

[2] https://www.mayoclinic.org/healthy-lifestyle/stress-management/in-depth/stress-symptoms/art-20050987

[3] https://www.nhs.uk/mental-health/self-help/tips-and-support/mindfulness/

[4] https://journals.sagepub.com/doi/abs/10.1177/0956797615593705

[5] https://journals.sagepub.com/doi/abs/10.1177/0956797612449176

[6] https://pubmed.ncbi.nlm.nih.gov/20671334/

[7] https://www.theatlantic.com/health/archive/2015/07/mindfulness-meditation-empathy-compassion/398867/

[8] https://www.psych.ox.ac.uk/research/mindfulness

[9] https://archive.nytimes.com/well.blogs.nytimes.com/2011/01/28/how-meditation-may-change-the-brain/

[10] https://www.smh.com.au/lifestyle/relax--its-good-for-you-20090819-eqlo.html

[11] https://journals.sagepub.com/doi/abs/10.1177/1948550614559651

Chapter Four

[1] https://auraglow.com/blog/benefits-of-smiling/

[2] https://e360.yale.edu/features/ecopsychology-how-immersion-in-nature-benefits-your-health

[3] https://www.nhlbi.nih.gov/health/sleep/why-sleep-important

Chapter Five

[1] https://central.gymshark.com/article/rise-and-shine-how-to-tap-into-your-brain-waves-for-an-effective-morning

[2] https://www.verywellhealth.com/morning-sunlight-exposure-3973908

[3] https://www.huffpost.com/entry/email-apnea-screen-apnea_b_1476554

[4] https://health.clevelandclinic.org/science-clear-multitasking-doesnt-work/

[5] https://www.theguardian.com/science/2008/mar/21/medicalresearch.usa

Chapter Six

[1] https://www.mentalhealth.org.uk/explore-mental-health/kindness/kindness-matters-guide

Chapter Eight

[1] https://www.sciencedirect.com/science/article/abs/pii/S0016718511000595

[2] https://positivepsychology.com/benefits-of-journaling/

Chapter Nine

[1] https://www.hsph.harvard.edu/nutritionsource/mindful-eating/

[2] https://www.webmd.com/obesity/features/slow-down-you-eat-too-fast

[3] https://www.healthline.com/nutrition/overeating-effects

[4] https://www.health.harvard.edu/blog/when-dieting-doesnt-work-2020052519889

[5] https://pubmed.ncbi.nlm.nih.gov/21977314/

[6] https://www.ncbi.nlm.nih.gov/pmc/articles/PMC5788730/

[7] https://pubmed.ncbi.nlm.nih.gov/24854804/

[8] https://betterhumans.pub/how-to-use-mindfulness-meditation-to-overcome-emotional-eating-aa95003cfe64

Chapter Ten

[1] https://www.healthline.com/nutrition/12-benefits-of-meditation

[2] https://nhahealth.com/brainwaves-the-language/

[3] https://www.manhattancbt.com/archives/309/how-long-should-you-meditate/

[4] https://www.psychologytoday.com/gb/blog/feeling-it/201409/18-science-backed-reasons-try-loving-kindness-meditation

Chapter Twelve

[1] https://www.sciencedirect.com/science/article/abs/pii/S0272735811000973

[2] https://www.latimes.com/science/la-xpm-2013-aug-08-la-sci-sn-meditation-may-help-reduce-smoking-20130806-story.html